Beating the Heat:
Why and How We Must
Combat Global Warming

Other Books by John J. Berger

Charging Ahead: The Business of Renewable Energy and What It Means for America

Ecological Restoration Directory of the San Francisco Bay Area (Ed.)

Environmental Restoration: Science and Strategies for Restoring the Earth (Ed.)

Nuclear Power: The Unviable Option, A Critical Look at Our Energy Alternatives

Restoring the Earth: How Americans Are Working to Restore Our Damaged Environment

Understanding Forests

Beating the Heat

Why and How We Must
Combat Global Warming

———

By John J. Berger

BERKELEY HILLS BOOKS
BERKELEY, CALIFORNIA

Published by
Berkeley Hills Books
P. O. Box 9877
Berkeley, California 94709
(888) 848-7303
www.berkeleyhills.com

Cover design by Elysium, San Francisco.
Illustrations by John Nelson
Manufactured in the United States of America.
Printed on 100% recycled paper.
Distributed by Publishers Group West.

1 3 5 7 9 10 8 6 4 2

To Nancy, Daniel, and Michael

Library of Congress Cataloging-in-Publication Data

Berger, John J.. 1945-
    Beating the heat : why and how we must combat global warming
    / by John J. Berger.
        p.cm.
    Includes bibliographical references.
    ISBN 1-893163-05-9 (alk. paper)
        1. Global warming. 2. Climactic changes. 3. Greenhouse effect,
    Atmospheric. I. Title.

QC981.8.G56 .B44 2000
363.738'747--dc21

00-024453

Contents

Acknowledgments

Research support for this book was generously provided by the Newton D. and Rochelle F. Becker Foundation and by Bill Roppenecker, president of Trace Engineering Co.

Research assistant and office administrator Jan Thomas assembled a treasure trove of information and contacts. Jan's successor, Andrew Perkins, tirelessly assisted in research, table preparation, proofreading, and referencing.

I owe a debt of gratitude to John Strohmeier of Berkeley Hills Books. That this book has kept its intended slender profile is very much a tribute to his editorial skill.

I owe a deep debt to Sierra Club staff members Dan Becker, Paula Carrell, and Bruce Hamilton and to Eric Wesselman of the Union of Concerned Scientists for helping me with the book's lobbying guide, policy chapter, and extensive list of resources (now available at www.berkeleyhills.com/beatingtheheat).

My warmest thanks as well to all of those listed below:

The members of my writing group, Bob Hall, Tom Brenner, Max Tomlinson, and Jerry Kramer. Also Newton D. Becker, Professor David King Dunaway, Thom Franklin, Langston James Goree VI, Chad Carpenter, Nancy Farr, Dr. Nancy P. Gordon, Professor John Harte, Paul Hesse, Dr. Andrew Horner, Peter Kelley, David King, Dr. Jon Koomey, Dr. Douglas N. Koplow, Dr. Florentine Krauss, Dan Lashof, Dr. Mark Levine, Robert Masterson, Alison Monroe, The Pacific Environment and Resource Center, Alan Sanstad, Dr. Matthias Schabel, and Professor Stephen H. Schneider.

My apologies to anyone I may have inadvertently left off this list.

Foreword

*B*eating the Heat is a book about global climate change. It describes what causes climate change, what its consequences are, and what can be done to prevent them.

Hope for maintaining a livable climate is justified. Safe energy technologies that can run the world's economy are available now. The resources they depend on are abundant. Power from these sources is clean and affordable—in many cases, cheaper than from conventional energy sources.

Given these realities, the world must begin the shift to renewable energy now. The stakes are awesomely high.

Victory in reducing our dependence on coal, oil, gas, and nuclear power gives us a chance to preserve a healthy planet for ourselves and our descendants. Defeat means we conduct a perilous global climate-change experiment on ourselves, the Earth, and all that is dear to us.

An enormous amount of work lies ahead if we are to limit global warming. Fortunately, ordinary people who are deeply committed to this goal can make a difference. They can thereby change the course of history.

Introduction

The amount of carbon dioxide in the air is a crucial determinant of future climate. If we go on adding carbon dioxide to the air at current rates, our climate will be profoundly disturbed. Why should that concern us?

Although unable to make exact predictions, scientists believe that our atmosphere's carbon dioxide level is likely to double over the next hundred years. With that doubling, the world's average temperature is likely to increase 2°- 6°F.

Then again, without corrective action, carbon dioxide levels might even triple by the year 2100. That could raise the world's temperature by 8° or 9°F. While that may not sound like much—after all, temperature can easily swing 30°F in a day—an average world temperature change of 9°F is all that separates today's benign climate from an Ice Age, when the place you now live may have been buried under two miles of ice.

Even if our production of airborne carbon is significantly reduced between now and 2100, global warming will not halt on January 1, 2101. Once disrupted, climate processes remain disturbed for hundreds of years. The oceans, for example, take centuries to release accumulated heat, and carbon we put in the air today remains there for up to 200 years, continuing to warm the planet. As the Earth's temperature rises, its living systems will inevitably be disrupted.

If you are not sure why we should care if a few more species go extinct, remember that nature is an interconnected fabric. Poke enough holes in it, tear it, yank on it hard enough, and it will rip. Once in ruins, it is very difficult and costly to mend, and the services it was unobtrusively providing are suddenly in jeopardy or gone.

These include services like purifying our air, cleaning our water, maintaining our soil, keeping pests in check, pollinating our crops, and providing us with the biodiversity from which medicines come. Of course, nature also offers us knowledge and insights about ourselves as an integral part of creation. If we destroy nature, we eventually destroy ourselves.

A metaphor provided by ecologist Paul Ehrlich illustrates why we must resist fervently when our environment is threatened or dismembered. Life, he proposes, may be likened to a flight on an airplane. Some of the passengers, each for their own good reason, greatly prize rivets and persist in removing them one by one from the plane's wings and fuselage.

With each extraction, the rivet poppers argue that a rivet's absence will make little difference. At first, the argument seems convincing, for the plane's operation is unaffected. Then, just one too many rivets is removed, and the plane suddenly crashes.

Like the passengers on that plane, we on planet Earth depend profoundly on nature in countless ways, even though our awareness of that dependency has dimmed as technology has insulated us from the natural world. Meanwhile, technology enables us to remove more rivets faster, and the strain of a swelling population on our resources increases the clamor for ripping out more rivets.

The world in which we live today is already under siege from many quarters. Rivets are popping furiously. The accumulating stress on the Earth is severely impairing its ability to adjust to assaults on its climate. Let's peer into the future and see what could happen next. Fasten your seat belts. And put on your crash helmets.

CHAPTER ONE

After the Warming

Global warming knows no geographic or national boundaries. An overheated climate affects all natural resources, all species, all people, everywhere. By altering sea level, temperature, and weather patterns, a rapidly changing climate forces grasslands, forests, farms, and wetlands to rearrange themselves on the landscape.

True, global temperatures have risen before and nature has adapted. In that sense, nature is indifferent to how ecosystems jockey for position across the Earth. But previous warmings of the magnitude now projected have taken place over millennia, not over decades or centuries. The natural world has had far more time to adapt to the new conditions. And neither superhighways nor urban sprawl halted those ancient migrations.

Moreover, in prehistoric times, the world's population was thousands of times smaller than the six billion people alive today. Human consumption of the world's natural resources was minuscule. By contrast, the natural resources on which today's huge population depend are already overexploited.

Under these conditions, how well would the natural world take the gigantic additional stress of a sudden climate change?

Scanning the Earth in the Year 2100

Imagine that you are a journalist who went to sleep in the year 2000 and awoke in 2100. You had a hankering back then to cover what you suspected would be the greatest story of the coming century, perhaps of all recorded history. So you recruited medical scientists to put you into a safe, trancelike state of suspended animation.

Colleagues at a large foundation set up a trust fund on your behalf. Under their sponsorship, interim care was provided, and they arranged for you to have the best available technology for assessing the state of the world upon your awakening. While you slept, the world warmed, and global population swelled to 11 billion people.

It is now August 1, 2100, and a bright, unseasonably hot morning Sun is streaming in your window. The powerful rays graze your eyelids and dazzle you awake on schedule. The world's average temperature rose more than 6°F while you snoozed.

Splashing your face with lukewarm water from the cold tap of your faucet, you rub your eyes and prepare to set off to see how the world has changed. Thanks to the march of technology, you have at your disposal a personal transportation device (PTD). Like the fishing rod that you're taking to combine business with pleasure, the PTD is made out of light, sturdy carbon fibers. It takes off and lands vertically, like a helicopter, and can jet around the planet at supersonic speeds. The PTD can travel with lightning agility on highways or on roadless terrain and skim over water like a hovercraft.

Along with your other gear, you pack Jenny, a hand-held, voice-activated computer. Whenever you notice anything of interest, you can query her for information, and she will retrieve almost anything from the greatly expanded Internet. Over your protein-powder-shake breakfast, you lay out your itinerary. You will tour North America first before heading to other continents. New England will be your first stop.

As you fly over New York and Connecticut, you notice dead and sickly evergreens at higher elevations. You set your PTD down in Massachusetts where, as a child, you used to fish for brook trout, rainbows, and browns. No matter where you cast your line here, however, none of these fish rise to your fly. You place your hand in the stream. It's tepid now—too warm for trout.

Once aloft again, you query Jenny about northeastern forests. You learn they have been infested with pests and diseases that thrive in warmer conditions. Higher temperatures have also accelerated the formation of ozone, which eats away at plant tissue. The trees in this region are dropping their leaves early. The sugar maples of Vermont have packed up for Maine.

Curious to see what's happened farther north, you head your PTD in that direction. You recall from your college days that about half of North America's wetlands are in Alaska, the Yukon, and the Northwest Territories. Most of them rest on permanently frozen ground. Climatologists a century ago predicted that within fifty years the southern edge of this permafrost would move 300 miles north.

You begin to see that the permafrost has indeed melted, and the ground has slumped over vast areas. Large amounts of sediment have sloughed off the land into streams and rivers. Patchy wetlands, lakes, and ponds maintained by ground ice have drained.

Jenny confirms that peatlands have also disappeared across much of the MacKenzie Basin. These ecosystems had built up carbon-rich deposits of organic matter thirty feet deep. Now dried out, the peatlands are releasing their stores of carbon dioxide, further adding to global warming. You choose the Queen Maud lowlands for a closer look.

The flat plain of the southern Arctic ecozone to which the Queen Maud Gulf area belongs was world famous in the twentieth century for its unspoiled natural beauty. The treeless tundra was the summer range for caribou herds. Bear, wolf, and moose roamed widely. Ducks and other migratory birds nested in large numbers. Falcons patrolled the skies. Snowy owls feasted on lemmings and arctic ground squirrels. The Inuit people hunted in this wildlife paradise.

As you reach what was once the center of the area, you are shocked. The whole regional ecosystem is virtually gone from the mainland of North America. It is as if summertime heat, like a giant blow drier, has parched the once-extensive wetlands. Fires have burned some of the bogs, and spindly trees have crept in from the south. Wildlife is scarce. The Inuit no longer live here.

In hopes of finding something pure and unspoiled, you head further north to visit the Arctic Ocean. From the smattering of geology you picked up in school, you know that ice nine feet thick has covered an area here the size of the United States since time immemorial. Looking down from aloft, however, you see that huge areas of the Arctic are now ice-free. You search in vain for the seals, walruses, and penguins that used to live here in large numbers.

You check your position and confirm that you're still on course. "What's happened here, Jenny?" you ask.

The Earth's polar ice began disappearing more than a hundred years ago, she responds. As early as the 1990s, in fact, a chunk of ice the size of Rhode Island broke off the Antarctic Peninsula, in the southern hemisphere. Ice gradually began forming later in the fall and melting earlier in the spring. The more the ice melted, the more open water was exposed to the Sun. Unlike ice, water is a great heat-absorber. The more the ice melted, the warmer the region became. The ice disappeared faster and faster.

You shift your route southward again, piloting your PTD low across the vast permafrost region of Canada where scrawny trees now tilt at crazy angles in the soft Earth. The northern forests beyond them appear dry, some burned, some sickly, some already dead.

In south-central Canada, you discover corn growing far outside its previous range. Jenny tells you that soils have grown drier in the Midwest, and that U.S. wheat, corn, and soybean production have moved north into the Great Plains and southern Canada. In the southern U.S., corn and soybean yields have fallen so low that farmers have shifted to fruits and vegetables. Demand for irrigation water has soared almost everywhere.

Approaching the Great Lakes, you see that they have sunken deeply in their basins and that water flow into the St. Lawrence Seaway is low. You learn that during the hotter, drier summers, scarce runoff has made navigation difficult. If the interior is so dry now, what is happening along the coasts? Your family used to have a beach house on Cape Cod. You point the PTD's nose eastward.

Soon you land in a field on the outskirts of Cape Cod and taxi down a once-familiar road toward the beach. It doesn't lead there any longer. Waves are lapping over the shore where you played as a child. Here and there, building foundations protrude from the surf.

With some trepidation, you consult Jenny. You learn that during the twentieth century, sea level along the North American coast rose 4-10 inches. But global warming in the past one hundred years has greatly accelerated the process. The sea on the average has risen another twenty inches.

Airborne again, you head south along the coastline of Rhode Island, Connecticut, New York, and New Jersey—territory you've traveled many times. Looking down, you notice that few coastal wetlands are left. Long stretches of these shores used to have wide, green ribbons of salt marsh on their seaward side.

Half of the nation's coastal wetlands have been flooded by the sea in the last hundred years, Jenny tells you. They've been trapped by the seawalls and bulkheads that have been built to protect property from flooding. The fishing industry is in big trouble, too, she adds. You ask her for more details.

Wetland plants require a specific range of elevations relative to sea level to survive, Jenny informs you. As seas rise, these plants retreat inland, propagating their way to higher ground. But because of roads, levees, and landfills, wetland migration has been cut off along much of the East Coast. More than half of the commercial fish species use wetlands during their life cycle, she adds. The fishing industry is in a permanent depression.

Your PTD approaches the expanse of Chesapeake Bay, once home to crab and oyster fisheries. You cruise low over the water but can't see what's going on below the waves because the water is so murky. Frustrated, you call on Jenny again.

She reports that the famous Chesapeake Bay oyster populations have dwindled, badly hurt by the bay's dirty water and increased salinity. Small oyster farms have been driven out of business. And along the shores, sea water has intruded into fresh water supplies. Urban water intakes have had to be moved farther up the Potomac River. The bay's smallest islands have disappeared. The larger ones have shrunk.

As you head farther south, you see waves where islands once buffered Virginia from heavy seas. The Outer Banks of North Carolina, including the Cape Hatteras barrier, are virtually gone. Albemarle and Pamlico Sounds are now exposed to the full force of Atlantic storms that once would have spent their fury on the lost barrier beaches.

You toss Jenny the word "storm," plus "sea level rise," and she comes up with these facts: Sea level rise has been accompanied by more severe storms over the past hundred years. The danger from higher seas is therefore multiplied. Higher storm surges pour over seawalls and levees. Floods that used to happen once a century now occur more frequently.

North Carolina seems to have lost 1,000 square miles to the sea. Wars have broken out, you reflect, when one nation has taken even a few miles of land from another. But it appears that the United States has given up thousands of square miles without a fight. The sea has stolen it quietly, inch by inch.

As you proceed south, the map of the southeastern U.S. has been further redrawn. Thousands of square miles are under water here, including the Florida Keys and much of Everglades National Park. Further inland, the vegetation appears far more tropical than you had thought possible at this latitude. After all, you wonder, doesn't the Tropic of Cancer run just north of Havana? Jenny quickly confirms this. So some of the subtropics have turned into tropics. As you try to comprehend this, tropical illnesses come to mind.

From the Internet, Jenny informs you that malaria, yellow fever, and bonebreak fever have once again become prevalent in Florida as warmer temperatures have pampered disease-carrying mosquitoes. Tourists and retirees have been shunning Florida. More vigorous mosquito-control efforts have not cured the problem, as pesticide-resistant mosquito strains have become widespread.

You now leave the Florida coast to see what has happened to the low-lying parts of Louisiana and Mississippi. Jenny now anticipates the information you want and provides facts. In the 1990s, the area supported a third of the nation's $2 billion a year commercial fish and shellfish catch. Now much of the Delta is flooded. Coastal pipelines and other infrastructure are half underwater. Jenny pulls a study off the web. It reports that spotted sea trout, oysters, and flounder have lost "most, if not all, of their habitat."

She informs you that New Orleans was 6.5 feet below sea level a century ago, and has since sunk several feet more. The sea has risen a record 4.5 feet in Grand Isle, about 45 miles south of New Orleans. Flooding is a big problem everywhere in bayou country.

Onward you go to the gulf coast of Texas where Jenny reports sea level has risen more than a yard. Galveston has spent billions reconstructing its seawall. As seas have risen along the Texas Gulf, eliminating its wetlands, birds, fish, and shellfish have disappeared. The state's brown shrimp catch, once so economically important, is trivial now, and many fishing people have lost their livelihoods.

You cross the southwestern U.S. and enter California, traversing the baking Mojave and Colorado deserts. Heading toward the populated southern coast, you fly over two large wildfires burning out of control across brushy hills, consuming luxurious homes built along the bone-dry canyons. Jenny tells you that even though summer fires were not uncommon in California's Mediterranean climate one hundred years ago, hotter weather and drier soils have made blazes far more frequent and severe.

Turning back toward California's Central Valley, you see miles of once-productive land standing idle. You come to a large concrete aqueduct and trace it from the air back to a large, half-empty reservoir. Evidently, supplies are insufficient to irrigate all the acreage that needs water while meeting expanded urban demands. Continuing north, you see more partially dry reservoirs and wonder how the state will get through the summer and fall.

Jenny does a search for you, and you learn that while winter runoff has increased, spring and summer runoff has dropped. The reservoirs are too small to hold enough of the larger winter flow to make up for the summer shortages. Water now becomes scarce in California just when farms need irrigation most. Wild salmon populations and other cold water species that need high spring flows have been decimated.

Flying north toward San Francisco Bay, it appears that rising seas have not only flooded bayfront property, but have also invaded the freshwater marshes of the Sacramento-San Joaquin Delta, crucial to the state's water supply system. A wedge of sea water has traveled far upstream. Evidence of submerged roads and bridges throughout the Delta are visible from the air. A dike system that once held river water back from the low-lying islands has long been breached, too, submerging rich delta farmland.

Tiring from your journey, you decide to check the Pacific Northwest before resting for the night. As you travel north, the changes you see along the coastlines and in the forests are familiar. A pattern of earlier snowmelt similar to California's has left less water available in summer and fall to produce adequate hydropower, on which the region's economy depends. Stream flows are too low at times for fish, and as in California, stocks are in worse shape or extinct.

You take a short detour to survey Mount Rainier, where you hiked as a youth through splendid alpine wildflower meadows. Landing on a small gravel road on the mountain, you step out and search vainly for meadows, finding that trees have invaded where the penstemon, primrose, and white heather used to grow. You stop in at the ranger station and learn that wildflowers on mountain tops everywhere have been displaced as warmer weather has allowed trees to ascend and conquer meadows.

After spending the night at a nearby inn, you are curious to see other parts of the world. You head westward across the Pacific. First, as a precaution, you decide to check on the health risks you may face.

After scanning several web sites, you find a map that shows where mosquitoes are now able to transmit malaria. Malarial mosquitoes survive only where winter temperatures exceed 61°F. Chillier temperatures kept them in check during the twentieth century in the temperate zones and at higher elevations. But because of global warming, the area of potential infection has now expanded as the disease has spread north and to higher elevations. Malaria now threatens sixty percent of the world's residents. Hundreds of millions of people are being infected each year, and millions are dying.

A rash of other tropical diseases is striking more victims, as well. These diseases include bonebreak fever, river blindness, encephalitis, cholera, yellow fever, and waterborne intestinal diseases. Rising temperatures, which speed up spoilage, have also caused worldwide increases in the incidence of salmonella from contaminated food.

Armed with this knowledge, you intend to stay aboard the PTD as much as possible. You decide that your first stop will be the Pacific island of Kiribati, then on to Tuvalu, then to the Marshall Islands. But when, one-by-one, you reach their exact coordinates and look down, you discover that they all have disappeared into the sea. The same thing happens as you search for other "stepping stones" in the Pacific. Finally, you reach some of the larger Solomon Islands that have survived. Reduced now in size, portions of the remaining dry land have been evacuated.

Your flight path is aimed toward central Japan now, but as you approach you see a huge storm on the horizon. Jenny tells you that the storm is a Class 5 tropical hurricane heading for Tokyo. Two previous Class 4 storms, she adds, which hit Japan earlier this year, did $150 billion in damage. This storm alone, she projects, is capable of wreaking $100 billion worth of havoc. You decide to avoid Tokyo and veer south.

This detour will give you an opportunity to view the spectacular coral reefs of the region. You slow your craft now and zoom in a few feet above the waves to explore the reefs between Kyushu and the Ryukyu Islands. Using special goggles that permit you to peer through the water, you observe that the reef is a bleached and unnatural white. Much of the coral appears to be dead. In place of the schools of multicolored tropical fish and anemone, the reef is almost deserted.

You poll Jenny for information and learn that when coral is stressed, it expels the algae that live within its tissues and dies. Multiple factors cause this—higher water temperatures, severe storms, sedimentation, freshwater inflows from heavy downpours, and contamination. You learn that forty percent of the world's coral are now dead or badly damaged.

You gain altitude again and steer toward north China. As you fly into the Yangtze Valley, refugee camps stretch as far as the eye can see along the edges of what appears to have been an enormous flood zone. You seek help from Jenny and learn that a colossal flood on the Yangtze River last year made 250 million Chinese temporarily homeless. Many have since relocated or rebuilt dwellings in the flood plain, but about thirty million have nothing to go back to and remain in refugee camps—as if the year-2000 population of California had suddenly been driven from their homes. Ironically, despite the huge earlier flood, the north of China is now parching—more of the extraordinarily wet winter plus dry summer syndrome.

How prevalent are disasters on this scale? Jenny does the research on recent floods. In the past year, several million people have been displaced from the coastal zones of Myanmar, Thailand, and Viet Nam, as well as Indonesia, the Philippines, and Malaysia. Bangladesh, meanwhile, is still two-thirds under water from an extraordinarily severe monsoon, which essentially halted its economy.

You now proceed south and west toward Africa, warned by Jenny that the continent has experienced the world's worst climate change impacts.

Back in the twentieth century, Africa was already ecologically ravaged. Tropical forests were being destroyed, wildlife exterminated, water resources depleted, and many grasslands were turning into deserts. The continent was largely dependent on rainfed agriculture for food and exports. The vagaries of nature even a hundred years ago were sending millions of Africans to urban centers. Jenny reveals that the situation has deteriorated badly since then. Population has expanded faster than economic growth while natural resources have declined.

Your first port of call is Egypt. A large part of its Nile Delta has been lost to rising seas through the combined effects of flooding and erosion. Sea level rise delivered the nation a two-fisted blow, reducing economic production while creating a crush of impoverished environmental refugees to be cared for in the cities.

Soaring now along West Africa's coast, you see that few of the affected nations have had the money to defend themselves against the sea, though many have large, low-lying cities on the coast. Severe flooding and heavy economic and human losses have resulted. Since rainfall has diminished and become less predictable, crop failures and famine are now even more frequent. Reduced water flows are also concentrating pollution and forcing water-dependent industries to shut down for months at a time.

The combined effects of environmental degradation and water scarcity have gravely damaged national parks and wildlife refuges on which tourism depended. Coastal resorts are now undesirable to travelers as beaches have disappeared and flood dangers have risen. Tourist-dependent cities have withered. The continent's economy is crippled.

You now decide to end your journey with a brief look at Europe, where you hope that wealth, foreknowledge of climate change, and advanced technology have staved off the worst impacts of global warming. After resting for a day in Tunisia, you fly across the Mediterranean to Greece, which looks especially barren and desiccated. Jenny confirms that Greece suffers from chronic water shortages.

In Italy's low-lying Po River plain and around Venice, which was built on a lagoon, you see construction crews hard at work elevating some already towering flood barriers. Flying over the Alps, you look in vain for glaciers. Here and there, a few small pockets of ice remain in cool, sheltered areas. They seem almost a mockery of the majestic mountains of ice that drew millions of tourists to Austria, Italy, France, and Switzerland.

The melting of the glaciers and high elevation permafrost, has aggravated mountain slope instability. Landslides are common now after almost any heavy rain. Some downslope villages have been abandoned. From Jenny, you learn that alpine temperatures have increased more than 7°F over the past century and that, as a result, mountain snow packs, too, have declined across Europe. Changed precipitation patterns have produced earlier spring peak river flows and lower river flows in the summers. The Rhine has dropped significantly, and runoff has declined by 30-35 percent in Hungary.

Flying over the Netherlands, you see that the extensive interior wetlands are quite dried out now. All along the developed shorelines, coastal marshes, too, are greatly reduced. The Dutch, longtime foes of the sea, have erected massive new flood barriers. Similar upgraded shoreline defenses can now be seen from the air around Hamburg and London.

Although there are still many places you haven't been able to visit, you are growing weary of the devastation climate change has brought and yearn for home. But with a start, you realize that you can never go back to the places you knew and loved. They and the world have been irrevocably changed.

With a pang of sorrow, you wish that in the twenty-first century, when opportunities for averting catastrophe still existed, you and others had taken steps to halt global warming.

The scenarios described in this imaginary journey are not fantasy, nor absolutely certain. They are reasonable projections, rooted in the best contemporary science. As you will see in the next chapter, many of them are based on global warming effects already observed today. They need not all come to pass if we set to work now to combat global climate change with determination and a willingness to devote the resources required to meet the challenge.

Let's now leave the realm of conjecture and briefly explain how our climate works and how we are disturbing it.

CHAPTER TWO

Heat-Trapping Gases and Our Climate

What determines climate, our average long-term weather?

Quite simply, the answer is, "Everything on Earth—plus the Sun." Climate results from interaction between the Earth and the flood of solar radiation in which it basks. Once we understand more about how climate operates, we can then answer questions such as:

What causes global warming?

What could trigger a rapid and dangerous climate shift?

How close are we to pulling that trigger?

To begin our search for answers, let's first see how our climate is set in motion by the Sun.

The Sun's Prodigious Energy

Vast quantities of energy spew out of the Sun and pour over the Earth. The Earth shuffles the energy around and sends it flying back into space. This solar energy keeps the planet's temperature far above freezing, powers the winds, and produces ocean waves. It also provides the energy that lifts water into the air by evaporation, and thereby makes precipitation possible.

How can a body 93 million miles away control our climate?

Answer: The Sun is unimaginably large, containing 99.8 percent of all the mass in our solar system. Every second, it crushes 700,000,000 tons of hydrogen in its core into helium and energy. The amount of energy produced is beyond ordinary comprehension. Phrases like "billions of watts" do not begin to describe it.

As the Sun's energy reaches the fringes of our outer atmosphere, it begins to encounter an obstacle course of gas molecules, dust, and clouds. Most of the Sun's radiation is then absorbed or scattered back into outer space or toward the Earth by the atmosphere and clouds. However, about a quarter of the Sun's incoming light misses clouds, dust, and opaque molecules. This is the direct beam radiation we perceive as bright sunlight.

Of the Sun's energy that reaches the Earth's surface some is reflected, and about half is absorbed by waters, land, and vegetation. As the energy is absorbed, it heats these surface features and is transformed into infrared radiation, which radiates skyward.

This infrared radiation must again pass through a gauntlet of gas molecules, dust, and other tiny particles in order to leave the atmosphere. Among the gas molecules that it encounters in the atmosphere is carbon dioxide. Just as clear glass transmits visible light while a dull black piece of metal absorbs it and heats up, atmospheric gases are not all equally transparent to radiation. Each gas absorbs, transmits, or reflects radiation differently. Carbon dioxide and other heat-trapping gases happen to absorb infrared radiation much more readily than visible light. These gases intercept the outgoing infrared energy, blocking its escape from the Earth.

As the heat-trapping gases absorb infrared energy, this warms the atmosphere. Some of that energy reradiates earthward again, so that it ricochets back and forth between the Earth and the atmosphere. The longer the solar energy remains trapped here, the warmer the Earth gets.

Climate Cycles

The temperature of the Earth is controlled by the ratio of incoming to outgoing radiation. When the two are in balance, the net heat loss or gain is zero. The Earth's climate, however, is not constant. For a long while, the Earth may gain energy from space, and the Earth's temperature increases. Then, for another long stretch, the Earth's temperature drops as radiation escaping the atmosphere exceeds radiation arriving from space.

Prolonged periods of substantial cooling result in Ice Ages, when some parts of Earth may be covered by layers of ice up to five miles thick. During warming periods, much of the planet's icy mantle melts. Ice sheets retreat toward the poles, and vegetation and animal life expand northward and southward.

The Earth is currently in a warm interglacial period. But don't throw your winter parka away. Glaciers are likely to advance again sometime in the future—thousands of years from now.

What happens in our solar system to cause the Earth's dramatic long-term temperature cycles?

Anything that alters the amount of solar energy flowing to the Earth, such as a change in the Earth's tilt, wobble, or orbit around the Sun, could bring a substantial change in the Earth's temperature. All three variables do go through long-term changes known as "Milankovitch cycles" that regularly increase and decrease the energy reaching us. Whenever all three cycles coincide to accentuate the amount of sunlight hitting the globe's far northern or southern regions, the Earth appears to enter a warm period, such as we have enjoyed for the past 10,000 years or so.

These cycles thus may be responsible for causing climate to change profoundly from glacial to interglacial warm periods. I use the words "may be" because not all scientists accept this hypothesis.

We clearly have no influence over how much energy the Sun radiates or over the tilt of the Earth, the wobble of its spin, or its orbit. But we can greatly affect the composition of our atmosphere, which also has a powerful influence on our climate.

Mucking Up The Atmosphere

The atmosphere is a thin, gaseous film veiling the Earth. It consists almost entirely of nitrogen and oxygen. Mixed in are small amounts of carbon dioxide, methane, ozone, and other gases. Ninety-nine percent of the atmosphere is within eighteen miles of the Earth's surface. Seen from space, the near-Earth atmosphere is an astonishingly shallow layer, similar in its relative thickness to the Earth as an orange rind is to an orange.

One way we affect the atmosphere is by releasing carbon-rich and nitrogen-rich gases. In burning coal, oil, and natural gas, and by removing forests, which absorb carbon dioxide, we add about eight billion tons of carbon to the atmosphere annually. As explained, gases containing carbon slow the escape of energy from the atmosphere and cause it to get warmer. Although it is a misnomer, this warming process is often called "the greenhouse effect," and the gases that produce it are commonly known as "greenhouse gases."

The most important of these gases is carbon dioxide, which is produced anytime a carbon fuel burns or when any living thing breathes. The other leading heat-trapping gases influenced by humans are methane (the main component in natural gas), nitrous oxide (a component of auto exhaust), the halocarbons (which include some refrigerants), and ozone (that acrid smell produced by some air purifiers).

In addition to the burning of fossil fuels, such as coal and gasoline, human activities that add these gases to the air include raising livestock, manufacturing cement, producing certain industrial chemicals, dumping waste in landfills, and deforestation.

Some heat-trapping gases, like carbon dioxide, methane, and nitrous oxide, are naturally present in the air. We're just adding a great deal more of them to it. Other gases, for example, the halocarbons, were unknown until they were synthesized for industrial use.

Carbon Dioxide, Earth's Thermostat

Although carbon dioxide makes up only a tiny fraction of the atmosphere and is not the most powerful heat-trapping gas, it is more responsible for changing our climate than any other gas we produce.

"Greenhouse Gases"

I prefer to use the term "heat-trapping gases" when referring to carbon dioxide, methane, nitrous oxide, and other synthetic "greenhouse gases." The greenhouse analogy can be misleading.

A greenhouse readily admits visible light. Once inside, some of this solar energy is reflected outward; the rest is absorbed and reradiated as heat, which warms the soil, plants, and air molecules. The glass skin of the greenhouse then keeps the plants warm by preventing the movement of warm air molecules out of the greenhouse—a process known as convection.

Unlike a greenhouse, heat-trapping gases do not warm the Earth by preventing convection. They heat the Earth by continuously absorbing and reradiating solar energy that otherwise would have escaped to space had it not been intercepted.

A more serious problem with the greenhouse metaphor is its warm, comfortable connotation. By contrast, disruption of global climate is far from a "feel-good" experience.

This is because we add more of it to the atmosphere—by far—than any other. Amazing as it may seem, by adding only a few hundredths of a percent of it to the air, we change our climate.

The Earth's temperature and the concentration of carbon dioxide in the atmosphere have risen and fallen together for at least the past 420,000 years—as far back in time as our instruments can probe. This is extraordinary evidence for an intimate connection. Only in the past 150 years, however, have human actions actually begun markedly raising the carbon dioxide levels in the atmosphere.

Before the Industrial Revolution, the Earth's atmosphere had about 280 parts per million (ppm) carbon dioxide. Currently the concentration is about 370 ppm. So just since the early nineteenth century, the concentration has increased by about a third. Meanwhile, over the past one hundred years, the mean temperature of the Earth has increased by about 1°F.

The effect of atmospheric carbon dioxide can be seen very dramatically on Venus. Venus is closer to the Sun than is the Earth, so we'd expect it to be somewhat warmer. But the temperature of Venus is a furnace-like 900°F. This is due primarily to the atmosphere of Venus, which is ninety-five percent carbon dioxide—more than 10,000 times the carbon dioxide concentration of the Earth's atmosphere.

Scientists believe that more than sixty-five percent of the warming that has occurred on Earth over the past century has been caused by carbon dioxide humans have added to the atmosphere. The concentrations of heat-trapping gases are now at their highest levels in at least 420,000 years.

Once carbon dioxide is in the atmosphere, natural processes slowly remove it. On the average, removal takes 50-200 years. But that is not the end of the carbon dioxide problem.

Unlike the other heat-trapping gases, carbon dioxide is not destroyed in the atmosphere. When a molecule of carbon dioxide vanishes from the air, it is redistributed to other carbon reservoirs. In each of these "carbon sinks," its fate is put on a distinct timetable by the natural processes operating in that part of the carbon cycle.

If incorporated into plants, for example, carbon may be released in years to decades, when the plant decomposes. The carbon may then be entrapped in soils, but eventually, it is likely to find its way back again to the atmosphere.

Thus, some of the carbon dioxide we put into the air ultimately spends *thousands* of years intermittently circulating there before eventually sinking to its ultimate fate in the ocean sediments.

A Rogues' Gallery Of Heat Blockers

Although the other heat-trapping gases are destroyed in the atmosphere, they also have important effects on climate.

Nitrogen remains in the atmosphere as nitrous oxide for an average of 120 years, until it is chemically broken down by solar energy. Molecule-for-molecule, nitrous oxide has a warming effect 200 times larger than carbon dioxide. Pollution from power plants and internal combustion engines puts human-made nitrous oxide into the air.

Methane, produced in nature and through agriculture and other human activities, only stays in the atmosphere for a dozen years. However, it has a per molecule warming impact about ten times larger than carbon dioxide's.

Chlorofluorocarbons, the now-banned synthetic refrigerants, destroy vast quantities of ozone in the upper atmosphere, and exert a powerful heating effect on the Earth. CF_4, a synthetic compound, persists in the atmosphere for 50,000 years.

Sulfur hexafluoride, an insulating fluid for heavy electrical equipment, has a long atmospheric lifetime and thousands of times the warming effect, per molecule, of carbon dioxide. Fortunately, the quantities released are far less than those of carbon dioxide.

At high altitudes, where it is formed naturally, ozone is a significant heat-trapping gas. Nevertheless its presence there plays an essential role in limiting the amount of harmful ultraviolet rays reaching the earth, rays which can cause cataracts, skin cancer and mutations. In the lower atmosphere, where it is primarily of human origin, ozone is highly corrosive and a key element in smog.

Water vapor, another powerful heat-trapping gas, often coalesces into clouds in the atmosphere. Clouds have a profound effect on the climate. They shield and cool the Earth by day and warm it at night by intercepting outgoing thermal radiation. But the volume of water vapor in circulation is not significantly altered by humans.

Climate Coolers

Not everything we put in the air heats things up. Tiny airborne particles known as aerosols, which appear in the atmosphere as haze, are important in cooling the Earth. Aerosols are produced both by natural phenomena, such as volcanoes and dust storms, and by humans in burning fossil fuels.

These and other aerosols usually only remain airborne for days or weeks. Since they exert a short-term cooling effect on climate, aerosols tend to mask the dangerous, protracted warming effects of the longer-lasting heat-trappers that often accompany them.

Displaced Ecosystems and Carbon Dioxide

Biomes are regional ecosystems dominated by characteristic vegetation—forests, wetlands, prairie, savanna, tundra, and so forth. The boundaries of these regional ecosystems will shift in response to new climatic conditions and their secondary effects—changes in interspecies competition and predation.

Some biomes will be able to adapt to the direct and indirect changes, others will be displaced. But biomes do not move as a unit. Individual species within biomes will adapt or move at their own rates, creating new and sometimes novel assemblages of species.

The rapid pace of climate change would require that many biomes migrate ten times faster than their historical migration rates. Biomes unable to adapt would die and release significant portions of their stored carbon to the atmosphere. This would warm the atmosphere and further exacerbate global warming, an effect known as "climate change feedback." (See Appendix B: Frequently Asked Questions About Our Climate.)

True, the vanquished ecosystems, such as northern forests, would eventually be replaced by new biomes, such as tundra, better suited to the new climatic conditions. But, before that occurred, the atmosphere would receive a large dose of carbon dioxide as the now-unsuited biomes perish and decompose.

The Heat Is On

In the past century, the world's mean temperature has increased by about 1°F. The decade of the 1990s was the hottest since 1860, when instruments first began to be widely used to track temperatures, and seven of the ten warmest years on record occurred during that decade.

Climatologists believe that global mean temperature has not varied as much as 1.8°F within the previous 10,000 years, so the 1°F increase we have had in just a century is a very rapid one indeed. Many natural processes and events now show the effects of this increase in surface temperature.

- When the Earth warms, sea level rises because of ice and snow melt, and the thermal expansion of water. The seas have already risen 4-10 inches since the nineteenth century.
- Since 1900, a widespread melting of high-latitude glaciers has become obvious. About half the glacial ice in the European Alps has been lost in the past century. In Glacier National Park, eighteen glaciers have melted away since 1966, and within 50-70 years, scientists expect virtually all the park's sixty-five glaciers to be gone. In the Caucasus mountains, half of all glacial ice has been lost in the past century, and in the Andes, glaciers are retreating at a rate seven times faster than during the 1970s.
- Glaciers in the Himalayas are receding faster than anywhere else in the world. These glaciers, the world's largest mass of ice outside the polar regions, are the source for the Indus and Ganges Rivers upon which over 500 million people depend for water. High melting rates have already caused unprec-

edented flooding and mud slides in northern India. Glaciers could be entirely lost here as early as 2035, leaving people in parts of India, Nepal, China, Pakistan and Bhutan without adequate water for drinking, irrigation, or village life.

- In the Arctic Ocean, the area covered by sea ice decreased by about six percent from 1978 to 1995. In the Antarctic, almost 1,150 square miles of ice shelves collapsed over a one-year period in 1998 and 1999. One 850-square-mile iceberg now threatens shipping lanes.

- In Alaska, permafrost has warmed by about 3.5°F since the 1960s, causing the ground to subside 16-33 feet in parts of the state's interior. Barrow, Alaska now averages more than 100 snowless days in the summer—a twenty-five percent increase since the 1950s.

- Populations of the Peary caribou in the Canadian Arctic have fallen from 24,000 to 1,100 in just four decades due to changes in climate which have brought heavier snows and freezing rain, burying food supplies.

- The average temperature of the Antarctic Peninsula has increased 3-4°F since the mid-1940s, and in some seasons, temperatures are 7-9°F higher. Wildlife in the region has had to alter migration ranges to secure food, and the Adelie penguin population has declined by a third in the last twenty-five years.

- Rising seas have covered or are threatening low-lying islands in parts of the Pacific Ocean, including Samoa, Fiji, Tonga, Vanuatu, and Palau. Outlying atolls have had to be abandoned because of rising waters.

- Coral reef bleaching, a probable effect of ocean warming and other causes, is now present in the Caribbean, the Galapagos Islands, the Pacific Ocean off Mexico and Panama, the Florida Keys, and across the seas from Samoa to Africa.

Milder temperatures have contributed to the spread of

mosquito-borne diseases in Africa. Richards Bay, South Africa, for example, which was once malaria-free, had 22,000 cases in 1999. Malaria has also reached highland regions of Kenya and Tanzania where it was previously unknown.

- In the Andes Mountains of Colombia, disease-carrying mosquitoes that once lived at altitudes no higher than 3,200 feet have now appeared at the 7,200-foot level.
- Researchers in Germany have concluded that spring is, on average, arriving six days earlier than just thirty years ago, and that fall is occurring about five days later. In the north-eastern United States, studies have found that ice is covering lakes fifteen fewer days per year than it did three decades ago.
- In Central England, the average number of days above 68°F has increased from four in the nineteenth century to twenty-six in 1995. Temperature rise has been accompanied by plant and animal life-cycle changes elsewhere in the United Kingdom: earlier spring spawning of some amphibians, earlier egg-laying by birds, and a northward shift in bird migrations.
- From 1995 to 1999, the Atlantic Ocean spawned more hurricanes than during any other five-year period on record. The four Category 4 hurricanes in 1999 were the most ever in a single year.
- The two storms that struck Western Europe in January 2000 were the worst ever recorded, leaving more than 100 people dead and causing more than $5 billion in damages. Almost two-thirds of France was declared a disaster zone, six bell towers of Paris' Notre Dâme Cathedral were destroyed, and avalanches and forest losses were widespread.
- The year 1998 was the warmest on record. April to June of that year were the driest spring months ever measured in the states of Florida, Texas, and Louisiana. In May, San Antonio, Texas received eight percent of its normal precipitation.
- In the northeastern U.S., the late spring of 1999 was the driest

since temperatures began to be recorded. Agricultural disaster areas were declared in fifteen states, with losses in West Virginia alone expected to exceed $80 million.

- Financial losses from weather-related disasters in Canada have increased by twenty to thirty times in the past fifteen years. The rise in damages from ice and wind storms, floods and droughts far exceeds inflation and the growth in value of the country's infrastructure.

(For more international "hot spots" see the *Global Warming: Early Warning Signs* website, www.climatehotmap.org.)

Limits to Our Knowledge

The Earth's climate is not completely predictable. It depends on some processes that have well-defined outcomes, some that depend on chance, and some that are chaotic. Much is still unknown.

For example, we do not know enough about the possibility that the Antarctic or Greenland ice sheets might melt. These two ice sheets together constitute the world's largest fresh water supply and melting of even a small fraction of them could cause a very large and fast gain in sea level. The West Antarctic ice sheet alone holds ten percent of the world's freshwater and, if melted, would cause a seventeen-foot rise in seal-level worldwide.

Currently, scientists are unsure whether the Antarctic in general and the West Antarctic ice sheet in particular are gaining or losing mass. The state of "mass balance" for the Greenland ice sheet is not well known either, although recent observations point toward its thinning.

Because of all the unknowns and the enormous consequences of miscalculation, common sense dictates that we proceed with caution. That means we need to do everything we can to minimize the release of heat-trapping gases and to maximize their recapture. We'll address these issues in chapters five and six. Our next chapter, however, discusses some of the staggering financial consequences of rapid climate change.

CHAPTER THREE

Counting the Costs

Imagine a high-level meeting in Washington, D.C. a little over a decade from now. Senior U.S. government officials are grappling with climate change. The political costs of avoiding the problem have grown. The officials are trying to grasp its economic impacts in order to lay the groundwork for belated decisive action.

September, 2012
The White House

The uniformed Marine guard swung open the tall double doors to the cabinet meeting room and saluted the Commander-in-Chief.

"Ladies and Gentlemen," he said, "the President of the United States."

Although it was only 7:30 A.M., the full Cabinet was already assembled around the long, polished mahogany table, finishing their croissants and coffee.

Sitting with the cabinet secretaries were the Vice-President, joined by the head of the Office of Management and Budget, the Environmental Protection Agency Administrator, the President's Science Advisor, the National Security Advisor, the President's Press Secretary, his chief pollster, and various assistants for domestic affairs. Deputies and assistant secretaries opened attaché cases and rustled papers in a circle of chairs farther from the table.

A bulletin from the White House Office of Communications lay on the table with the newly released climate statistics. The world's releases of greenhouse gases were skyrocketing instead of tapering off as the Administration had promised in its first term. The morning newscasts would be carrying the story.

It was clear to the public now that the carbon dioxide reductions promised by the industrialized nations in the 1997 Kyoto Climate Protocol weren't materializing. And the weather this summer was maddeningly hot in the Capitol. At times the air was suffocating.

These conditions seemed to be locking public attention on climate issues, and people were more irritable about them now than in the 1990s, as though the heat had exhausted their patience.

"They're blaming us whenever the thermometer goes over 100° two days in a row, " the President had griped the previous day to Martin Lopez, his Science Advisor. "Is there something we can do to cool things off for a while? Maybe the Pentagon could seed a few clouds over the Washington Press Club?" he deadpanned.

The world's average temperature had been rising fast since the 1970s—a quarter of a degree last year alone. It may have just been an aberration, but if that continued, the world's average temperature would rise a disastrous 25°F by the end of the century. All the cable news commentators were speculating about it. To top things off, the hurricane season had opened a month early with a pair of super storms just when memories of the crippling drought of 2008 were fading.

The President patted a few backs, shook hands with the Vice-President, and took his seat. "As you know," the President began, "Senator Spurgis caused some shock waves on the Senate floor yesterday when he broke with us over climate policy. He's blaming us for the collapse of the Kyoto process and scoring points with the farmers and his insurance buddies. It's quite a home run for him."

"It would've been nice if he'd voted for Kyoto II when it came up on the Senate floor," the Vice-President quipped, to appreciative murmurs.

"According to Spurgis," the President went on, "we should press the developing nations still harder. But to do that, we've got to put our own house in order. The press is crucifying us, the environmen-

The Kyoto Protocol

The Kyoto Protocol was adopted by the parties to the United Nations Framework Convention on Climate Change in Kyoto, Japan on December 11, 1997. The Protocol's intent is to increase international efforts to control the release of heat-trapping gases into the world's atmosphere.

The Kyoto Protocol sets specific emission reduction timetables and targets for industrialized nations. It is not yet binding on developing nations, although they may voluntarily participate.

Under the Protocol's terms, signatories must reduce their emissions of six global warming gases by an average of five percent below their 1990 levels during a five-year period extending from 2008 through 2012. The reduction target set for the U.S. is seven percent.

As of November 30, 1999, 84 nations had signed the Kyoto Protocol, although only a handful had formally ratified it. The United States has signed the Protocol, but the U.S. Senate is currently opposed to its ratification. The full text of the Kyoto Protocol can be found on the worldwide web at www.unfccc.de.

talists are bailing out, and the insurance folks who got taken to the cleaners by Hurricane Arnold finally are starting to say we gotta be more proactive. The auto guys are prepared to go along now that everyone's finally getting on the low-emission-vehicle bandwagon.

"So today, I want to look at what this global warming is liable to cost. We're not going to talk about mitigating it. I just want to know what the threat really is if we continue business as usual. We'll have plenty of time next week to discuss policy.

"We're going to put some numbers on this thing. Then, when the energy-industry claims we're going to bankrupt the nation, we'll point to all the money that we're going to save by our approach."

"Bruce," the President went on, turning to his Energy Secretary, "would you chair the discussion for us?" Bruce Sievers had been the driving force that finally had gotten the President's ear and convinced him to take a fresh look at climate policies.

"Thank you, sir," Sievers replied. "I'd appreciate the opportunity to make a few brief remarks." The President nodded.

Sievers plunged in theatrically. "As we all know, if our society can't get these greenhouse gases under control, then, God help us, Mr. President, ladies, and gentlemen, we, our children, our grandchildren, and their descendants will have to pay. Not just with money but with the quality of their lives.

"But speaking of money, the studies I've seen say that in forty years the cost of climate change will be $260 billion to $400 billion a year. And that's what we're going to have to pay every year thereafter just to repair the damage to the U.S.[1] I've therefore asked each Cabinet secretary to tell us what this is going to mean in their area of responsibility. Roger, why don't you start?"

Roger Anderson, Secretary of Agriculture, came to the rostrum. He was a tall awkward man in his mid-fifties with thick, pale brown hair. "My first projections this morning are based on a 4.5° average domestic temperature increase," he began. "The economic estimates for this are all over the map. One guy in data analysis claims that global warming is good for us. He says we're going to be growing a lot more tropical fruit and gourmet vegetables. Then I've got people telling me that wine grapes won't grow in the Napa Valley anymore and that wheat, corn, and soybean yields in the Midwest are going to hell in a handbasket, pardon the expression.

"Now, we're on more solid ground when it comes to water projections. As the interior of the nation gets warmer, we may see ten times the number of severe droughts. As a result, food prices are expected to go up—maybe ten percent, maybe forty, maybe 100 percent—it depends on the climate model.[2]

"Farming communities that have been pumping ground water like there's no tomorrow, or farming without irrigation, may go the way of the draft mule and the wooden plow. Keep in mind that during the Dust Bowl era in the 1930s, temperatures in the Midwest were only about 1.8° warmer than they are today, and that was enough to send people fleeing to California."

Secretary Anderson paused to run the fingertips of his right hand through his hair to ward off a mosquito.

"With a boost of 4.5° in the *global* average temperature, average heartland temperatures in the U.S. are going up 7-9°, and when you start talking about *that* kind of temperature rise, suddenly everybody agrees we're going to have major agricultural losses.

"That's going to dramatically increase evaporation, and the lost water isn't automatically going to be replaced by extra rain. Soil and crops are going to dry out, unless you increase irrigation. But you can't do that everywhere. The Colorado River, for example, is all spoken for. And, under warmer conditions, you've also got plants that are more susceptible to heat stress, pests, and disease.

"Now, for developing countries," Secretary Anderson continued, "the agricultural impacts of climate change are less precisely known, but they're ominous. Some economists say that drought due to climate change is going to cost world agriculture something like $18 billion a year. The U.S. drought of 1988, however, caused $40 billion in damages and that's just one event, so I don't know where they come up with $18 billion.[3]

"Dollar losses outside the U.S. may be high, but the human impacts are going to be worse. Hundreds of thousands may lose their lives over this. Millions more will suffer—a hundred and fifty million people could become environmental refugees in the next two decades.[4]

"Look at North Africa and the Middle East. Parts of these regions are already hot and dry. They'll be hurt by further warming. South Asia leans heavily on agriculture, too, so they're also very vulnerable. Or take sub-Saharan Africa; sixty percent of the population there depends directly on agriculture. You've already got malnutrition and occasional famine. Further warming will only make food supplies more insecure."

"Make a note of that, please," the President said, addressing the Secretary of State. "Let's consider increasing food aid for Africa this year."

"Maybe some more funding for AID?" the Secretary suggested. The President nodded and turned toward Anderson.

"Let's talk more about domestic water supplies," the President said.

"I'll defer to Chuck on that," the Agriculture Secretary replied, yielding the rostrum to Charles Lynch, a haggard-looking former Governor of Iowa, now Secretary of the Interior.

"Well, let's start with the big picture," he said in a bold, sonorous voice.

"Demand for water is rising steeply worldwide; we all know that. Climate change will stress water systems even further. Water will get scarcer and more costly. Its quality may suffer. We may even see water wars in some unstable areas. Even without hostilities, increased tensions could raise defense costs, particularly in the arid and semi-arid world.[5]

"Here at home, if average global temperature rises 4.5°, our water supplies are likely to fall maybe ten percent, on the average. That's $7-11 billion right there in lost water. It's like evaporating money.

"Some regions would be hit harder than the national average," he continued. "Like Roger said, the Colorado's already oversubscribed. And in the Sacramento Valley, if regional temperature rises 7°, summer runoff would fall by more than half. Hydropower producers would lose billions more in revenue.[6]

"Finally, just a word about forests. A third of the world's forests are likely to experience major changes after carbon dioxide doubles. Temperate forests may expand, but all other forest types will decline by about ten percent.

"Keep in mind that forest diebacks are going to happen a lot more quickly than new forest creation, so losses will far exceed gains during the adjustment process. Also, forest diseases and pests will spread in the meanwhile. It won't be a pretty picture. Some kinds of forests are going to disappear altogether, and the new forests we all hope to see won't necessarily arise—they'll have to compete with other land uses.

"We could lose forty percent of the standing trees and brush in the Western U.S. and Great Lakes area over the next 100 years or so and 35-40 percent of our commercial wood. Hard to put a dollar value on it—our estimates range from $3.3 to 44 billion a year."[7]

"Of course," interjected Agriculture Secretary Anderson, "those numbers don't cover all the lost forest values—wildlife habitat and non-timber products, or the recreational losses."

"Right," said the Interior Secretary, "but bear with me one more moment. There's another big issue here. If carbon dioxide doubles, drought conditions and more frequent thunderstorms could increase the number of lightning-caused fires in the southwestern U.S. by sixty percent a year. We estimate that the burned area would expand by 140 percent."[8]

"What's that going to do to air quality?" the EPA Administrator asked.

"I don't think anybody's bothered to think about that," Anderson replied.

Sievers broke in. "We have a broad agenda this morning, ladies and gentlemen. I'd like us to hear from Health and Human Services now."

"If you don't mind, Bruce," the President interrupted, "We're hearing a lot of conflicting opinions about the possibility of more-powerful hurricanes, tornadoes, and what we used to call 'natural catastrophes,' before the climate started changing. What's our best thinking on this now?"

"Martin, I think that's your bailiwick," responded Sievers, demurring to the Science Advisor.

Lopez, a former college basketball star, draped himself over the podium. "Mr. President," he conceded, "the science is still a little unsettled on this point. But let me tell you what we *do* know. Hurricanes will develop more frequently and may be more severe as the tropical seas where they're spawned get warmer. But climate change will affect different regions unevenly, and our global models don't pinpoint exactly what's going to happen where."

Bill Herman stirred in his seat. He had just taken the helm at the Federal Emergency Management Agency last month, and this was his first cabinet meeting. "Excuse me one moment, Dr. Lopez," he ventured. "It's worth mentioning that if the hurricane-effect you suggest does occur, it could cause huge damages and cost thousands of lives. A Class 5 hurricane in Miami, New Orleans, Galveston, or Charleston could cost tens of billions of dollars. Hurricane Andrew in 1992 did $30 billion."

"Let me just jump in here for a moment," said Commerce Secretary Dunsmuir from his seat. Now that the continuity of Lopez' presentation had already been breached, his air time was fair game. "Hurricane Andrew bankrupted nine insurance companies. The ones that were left reduced their coverage or got out of those areas. You can see where I'm going with this. Some of what we now consider mighty financial institutions could be shaken to their roots by the losses that may be coming.

"With even the *risk* of bigger or more frequent storms, insurance premiums are going up and coverage is going to be withdrawn in places where it's especially needed. Once an area becomes uninsurable, new economic development will be stymied. Forget new resort hotels on the beach. In fact, forget any large shoreline real estate investment.

"Let me just pursue this for one minute more. If catastrophes become more frequent, the costs of fire protection and weather emergency response *services* will also grow. Taxes will have to go up to cover them."

The FEMA Administrator had been fidgeting in his seat as Dunsmuir spoke. "We're also looking at more-frequent widespread power outages," Herman interjected. "The kind where a line goes down, the rest of the system gets overloaded, and in two seconds the lives of hundreds of thousands of people are disrupted. We could see a barrage of lawsuits." He stopped talking suddenly and looked around the room uncomfortably, like a school boy who had spoken out of turn.

"I believe we ought to hear from Health and Human Services next," Sievers said dryly, attempting to forge ahead through his formidable agenda. "Dean Driscoll," he announced.

"Thank you," said Ellen Driscoll, the Health and Human Services chief, bustling to the lectern.

"I just have a few points, just a few," Dr. Driscoll began, pulling out a hefty skein of notes and adjusting her bifocals. The President gazed at her blandly. He could see her lecturing her classes at the School of Public Health in Berkeley, from which he had drafted her.

"A world that on the average is 4.5° warmer will have more heat waves and fewer extremely cold spells," Driscoll droned, reading from her notes. "Health experts generally agree that the number of lives to be lost from heart attacks and strokes due to the higher temperatures will far outweigh the number of lives that will be saved by avoiding deaths from freezing and hypothermia.

"Plus, higher temperatures worsen air pollution, which increases the rate of potentially deadly respiratory diseases, such as asthma and emphysema.

"I will leave the economics to others better versed than I, except to say that current economic studies of health impacts tend to focus only on the direct costs of excess deaths. These studies do not include the costs of deaths caused *indirectly* by the spread of mosquitoes, rodents, and other disease carriers, nor do they tally the costs of nonfatal, heat-related illnesses."

The Secretary of Defense unsuccessfully tried to stifle a yawn.

"Even with these exclusions, the economic impacts will be substantial. The Fankhauser study in 1995 projected that an average global temperature increase of 4.5° will cause 115,000 additional deaths per year in developing countries, 115,000 deaths," she repeated, "and 23,000 deaths in the OECD nations. Depending on the monetary value that economists ascribe to a human life, these health effects are calculated at $49-188 billion per year."

The President interrupted. "That's quite a range you've quoted. Is it forty-nine or 188?"

"Mr. President," Driscoll resumed, "at the low end of that cost spectrum, mortality damages for the U.S. are $5.8-10 billion, and $34 billion for the OECD. The $10 billion U.S. estimate assumes that the population would eventually "acclimatize" to increased temperatures. But, if the population does *not* acclimatize, U.S. damages from heat-wave deaths could be as much as $60 billion a year."[9] People began fidgeting and an epidemic of coughs rustled through the room.

"The estimated health costs of global warming also typically don't include the costs of exposing an extra 200 million people to the risks of contracting malaria." Driscoll continued. "That increased exposure due to global warming is likely to produce several million extra cases a year and tens of thousands of additional deaths.

"Other tropical diseases are also likely to increase their range under warmer conditions. In Indonesia, for example," she noted, "the number of bonebreak fever cases would quadruple."

"Thank you, Dean Driscoll," Sievers said.

"And, if I may, just one final point," she went on flipping hurriedly through her notes. "Many other tropical diseases are likely to become more common at higher temperatures, including diseases that arise from spoiled food, polluted water, and poor sanitation.

"Thank you, Dean," Sievers said again, a bit more firmly. A faint smile of triumph flitted across Driscoll's face as she picked up her notes. "I just also wanted to add that as more people become sick, the public costs of helping them will swell. Insurance premiums and fees for medical services also may climb—that's just a fact of supply and demand. . . ." Her words trailed off as she sat down.

On cue, Alan Dunsmuir now took command of the rostrum. He was a former Navy Admiral who had gone to Wall Street after resigning his commission and had served as a trade envoy to China before his appointment as Commerce Secretary.

"I know we're getting a little tired of hearing about sea level rise," he began, "but I feel well-suited to contend with it. I had to deal with swells in my previous career, and apparently I can't avoid dealing with them here either," he laughed and the audience chuckled.

"So, as oceans rise, we all know that a lot of very valuable coastal real estate will be lost. A forty-inch rise would swamp about 6,500 square miles of U.S. dry land, and another 6,500 square miles of the nation's wetlands—about half the total. The cost of protecting these areas between now and 2100 would be $73-111 billion.[10]

"States and local governments that can afford to do so will need to build and maintain sea walls and dikes. They'll also need to raise roadways and bridges, replenish eroding beaches, and keep salt water out of their drinking water supplies. Interest rates may be driven up by all the public borrowing needed to finance these new public works.

"At the same time, homes and businesses will be melting off local tax rolls, and people who depended on coastal resources for a livelihood may become unemployed. They'll then pay no income tax and, instead, draw on social services. Other taxes may have to rise to compensate for those lost revenues.

"In developing countries, with large populations concentrated along shorelines, coastal-protection costs could easily exceed the amount of foreign aid we can provide." The Commerce Secretary peered owlishly over the tops of his glasses at the Secretary of State. "Economic development will suffer," he declared ponderously.

"And one final thought. These economic snapshots don't really count some important human costs. Say that you're forced to leave your home because of rising seas and more frequent storms. Are you going to feel just as well off because someone hands you a check for your property? I don't think so. So, let's not forget that climate change has a human face, too. Thank you."

Sievers looked pensive and a trifle anxious as he called on EPA Administrator Livia Wright for her presentation. Wright had been an environmental specialist on Vice-President Sarnoff's senatorial staff before his move to the White House. She was hard driving and outspoken but was also known for her political savvy.

"My distinguished colleagues have covered the ground well," she began. "There's not much I can add, but I'd like to highlight one problem I see emerging as water shortages reduce stream and river flows in many areas. The remaining waters won't be able to accept as much municipal or industrial waste without exceeding our water-pollution control standards. Wastewater treatment plants will have to be built or upgraded. Domestically, the costs could be anywhere from $15-67 billion a year.[11]

"My second point pertains to air quality. Each winter, millions of square miles of the Earth are covered with mountain-high clouds of polluted air. When the Sun shines on this witches' brew, ozone and other delightful compounds form. Temperatures rise, ozone levels rise, and air pollution worsens. So we'll have to chose: either suffer the economic damages *caused* by the additional ozone, or pay the costs of *reducing* ozone levels.

"My agency estimates that if average global temperatures increases by 4.5°, the number of U.S. cities violating federal ozone concentration regulations will double. The costs of reducing the excess ozone would be anywhere from $3.5 to $27.5 billion a year.[12]

"We've already heard an excellent summary about forest impacts from the distinguished Secretary of the Interior. No one has spoken yet, though, about losses of living species. If I may, I'd like to briefly address that.

"Forests currently contain two-thirds of all the Earth's species. Ecologists have shown that large numbers of species will be driven out of existence just by the contraction of forests. At the same time, other changes will deliver many species a one-two punch. Case in point, as temperature increases 3.6°, 10-50 percent of all animals of the northern Great Basin mountains will become extinct.[13] The loss of species will cost billions of dollars a year, if you believe that economists can put price tags on things like species and ecosystems."

She sat down, to good effect, without drawing any conclusions, letting the facts she had presented speak for themselves.

"Now," said Secretary Sievers, "we'll conclude with some perspective on the impact climate change will have on fish and fishing."

The respected head of the National Oceanic and Atmospheric Administration, David Horton, took the rostrum. He was a gentle, studious-looking man who enjoyed the complete confidence of his boss, the Commerce Secretary.

"I'm afraid I have to admit to you from the get-go that climate change will have complex effects on world fishing that I cannot easily summarize. You see, some marine fish populations will increase due to warmer water and longer growing seasons, or by moving to areas where fishing pressure is reduced.

"Other fisheries may contract or collapse in response to changes in water temperature, currents, and freshwater inflows. The pervasive wetland losses we expect will also hurt fishing wherever fish have used wetlands for feeding, spawning, or raising young.

"The natural warming and cooling cycles in the Pacific known as El Niño/La Niña may be models for what higher temperatures may bring to certain regions. We don't know for sure. But we do know that the warm phase of these cycles in 1983 and 1997-1998 brought a drastic reduction in marine plankton. As plankton populations fell, fish populations plummeted. Salmon deserted the West Coast for chillier Alaskan seas. Shrimp production fell. The Northeast Pacific ecosystem was broadly affected.

"Generally speaking, the marine fishing industry is likely to be seriously disrupted on a regional basis as fish stocks redistribute themselves geographically. Because of the existence of territorial waters and exclusion zones, it may not always be possible for fishing fleets to follow the fish they're equipped to catch.

"Even where this isn't an issue, some fishing interests may be unable to muster the investment needed to catch new species inhabiting their customary fishing grounds. Ports and processing facilities located near current fish supplies may find themselves far from sources of fish. Economic losses due to changes in fish availability are likely to be passed on to consumers through higher prices.

"Inland catches of salmon and other seagoing fish may also suffer in some regions when smaller snow packs result in reduced spring and summer river flows,[14] and there would impacts on fresh water species, too, but that really isn't my province. I'll rest my case here."

"Very good," Sievers responded. "Now I'd like to make a few concluding remarks. The economic analyses presented here suggest that the developed nations will suffer annual damages equal to 1-3 percent of their collective Gross National Product, if carbon dioxide doubles.

"At two percent, climate change would cost developed nations some $2.4 trillion every decade. Developing nations would suffer losses ranging from 2-9 percent of their GNPs. Some studies have projected damages as high as $17-20 trillion over 50 years. So, we know the costs will be large, but not how large.[15]

"With these numbers as a backdrop, we can compare these costs to those of any climate-change adaptation measures we might propose. In short, we've made progress today and should be ready for the battle royal next Monday, when we'll reconvene to review the Administration's climate-change initiative.

"On behalf of the President, I want to thank you for contributing to this assessment. If there's no objection, we're now adjourned."

Let's leave the cabinet members now and take a brief look at why even their formidable cost estimates vastly underestimate the dangers of climate change and are therefore not be an adequate basis for setting policy.

Short-Term Perspective

Most of the economic studies referred to in this meeting extend no more than a hundred years or so into the future. Yet climate change will continue for hundreds of years *after* we stop adding excess carbon to the atmosphere.

If carbon concentrations continue to rise, warming over a period of say, 300-500 years, could easily lift global temperatures by 10°-32°F. Sea-level by then would rise 6.5-10 feet, swallowing huge portions of the world's coastal zone.

Expectation of Gradual Change

The economic studies also assume that climate will change in a gradual, orderly manner. Yet recent climatological research has found evidence of abrupt climate changes that, in the past, have occurred within as little as ten years.

Dramatic changes of this kind might occur, for example, if the North Atlantic "conveyor belt" circulation were halted, which could plunge western Europe into a climate similar to Iceland's.[16] (See Appendix B.)

Undetermined Costs

Damage estimates tend to focus on impacts that can readily be described in terms of money. Most of these impacts involve sectors of the market economy, such as agriculture, fishing, real estate, and finance. However, other harm—increases in human suffering, damage to ecosystems, and destruction of wildlife—is exceedingly difficult or impossible to translate into money in a meaningful way.

As Professor John P. Holdren once said, we must not become obsessed by counting the things that are easily countable instead of the things that count.

Utilitarianism

Another critical shortcoming of the economic studies cited proceeds from a fundamental weakness of cost-benefit analysis, which is based on the theory of Utilitarianism. Utilitarianism holds that things have value only insofar as they have a use for human beings. The underlying assumption is that the universe exists, above all, to serve human needs.

In such a system, a human's willingness to pay for something, or to accept compensation for its loss, are often used as the measures of its value. One example of the absurd results that follow from these assumptions is the way that economic analysis can treat the destruction of biological diversity.[17] Species that will be driven extinct thus may be valued according to their medicinal value, or by how much people would pay to save them, visit them, or even hunt them.

These "willingness-to-pay" valuations are based on the assumption that the value of a species is not an intrinsic property, but is something conferred on it by humankind, in proportion to how much use we can get from it. The universe, however, is not an object created for our pleasure. If a species goes extinct, no amount of money will unkill it. No form of life should be dependent on popularity contests, profitability, or polls for its continued existence.

The Question of Fairness

Another problem with cost-benefit analysis is that it neglects issues of fairness in the distribution of climate-change risks and benefits. Cost-benefit analyses assume that the total benefits and costs of an action can be averaged over all individuals in a society, or in the world. The analyst simply chalks up the total costs and benefits and, if the losses equal the gains, zeroes them out.

But in practice, the benefits of industrial development are disproportionately enjoyed in the wealthier nations, while costs are disproportionately borne in the less-industrialized developing world. If you were a farmer in Africa whose crops would no longer grow in your native region and you therefore could no longer feed your children, would you feel fine about it because wheat yields had simultaneously improved in Canada?

Choosing Affordable Alternatives

In contrast to the unacceptable costs described in this chapter, we will see in chapter five that the costs of lowering carbon emissions and protecting our climate are affordable. Moreover, in addition to protecting the climate, they produce public health and environmental benefits that could save millions of lives.[18] These steps include investments in energy-efficiency technologies, in new clean energy sources and transportation strategies, and in better agricultural and land-use practices.

These precautionary policies make so much sense that our failure to implement them vigorously now is not only reckless but foolish. What then stands in the way of adopting them? The first impediment is a body of myth about climate change. In the next chapter, I will explain who promotes these myths and why, and will give each of the principal myths a lie-detector test.

CHAPTER FOUR

Myths and Mythmakers

The oil and coal industries and some of their largest customers are conducting a sophisticated multimillion dollar campaign to convince the public that climate change is not a serious threat. The campaign opposes international cooperation to protect the world's climate.

The industries involved have succeeded in confusing tens of millions of people about climate change and in mobilizing opposition to the 1997 Kyoto Protocol. The U.S. has signed the agreement, but industry opposition greatly weakened it and to date has blocked its ratification. The Protocol calls on the industrialized nations to reduce their greenhouse gas emissions by only five percent by 2012, instead of the sixty percent or more needed to stabilize the atmosphere's carbon dioxide concentration. (See page 43.)

The industries behind the anti-Kyoto campaign include coal, oil, auto, electric, metal, chemical, paper, cement, and railroads. Their efforts have been joined by various anti-environmental groups. The members of this coalition seem to share the belief that the unbridled use of fossil fuels is a good thing. Thus, I refer to this diverse interest group as "the fossil fuel industry." The natural gas industry, however, is not linked with the oil and gas people on climate issues, for reasons I will explain shortly.

Why are multibillion dollar industries with many other things to do busying themselves opposing a consensus about climate change forged by the world's leading climate scientists? The executives of these companies live on this planet, too. They have children and grandchildren. Don't they care about the environment? Yes, *but . . .* they also have conflicting priorities.

Since they profit directly from the production and use of carbon-based fuels, they do not want fuel sales reduced. They regard the possibility of new taxes that would make fossil fuels more expensive as a threat to their prosperity.

They take an equally dim view of stronger clean air standards. Air pollution regulations impose pollution control costs on fossil fuel polluters. Even if those costs are ultimately passed on to consumers, higher costs restrain demand and siphon away revenue. And technologies that improve fuel efficiency also depress fuel demand. So the fossil fuel industry has a powerful vested interest in opposing these antidotes to climate change.

The industry and its allies have a long history of working effectively together to oppose clean air and water regulations, and fuel efficiency standards. During much of the 1990s, these industries spent millions of dollars hiring public relations firms, sponsoring industry-funded think tanks, and creating "astroturf" coalitions with misleading names that sound like grassroots organizations.

Using these surrogates, the oil and coal industry and their allies sent their message out through press briefings, Internet web sites, news releases, newspaper ads, conferences, email and petition drives, and direct contacts with editors, columnists, television correspondents, government officials and business leaders. In 1993, they successfully halted the Clinton Administration's effort to pass a modest tax on the energy content of fuels, which would have helped control carbon emissions.

Today they continue to lobby Congress to oppose domestic renewable energy and energy efficiency programs which they decry as "back-door implementation" of the Kyoto Protocol.

The main tactics of the fossil fuel industry's climate campaign are to sow doubt about climate science and fear of economic pain. To create fear, the campaign charges that limiting carbon emissions would be exorbitantly expensive and would therefore boost prices, hurt consumers, and make American industry uncompetitive abroad. To sow doubt, the fossil fuel industries take alleged "uncertainties" in climate science out of context, blow them up out of proportion, and use them to stir up skepticism.

If they discredit climate science, they destroy the rationale on which any sound public policy for combating climate change could be based. Once the industry has created enough doubt in the public's mind and has sown enough fears, industry then need not prevail on the merits of the scientific debate. They have won.

In this chapter, we will slip the window dressing off the coal and oil industries' campaign against climate protection policy. We will also discuss the climate views espoused by more moderate elements of the business community. Finally, we'll examine some of the industry's most basic climate change myths.

How Industry Puts Its "Spin" on Climate Change

To create doubt and fear, the fossil fuel industry often works through proxy organizations, and through individual "climate skeptics," who generally have no credibility on climate issues in the scientific community. These voices obfuscate the issues, paralyze the policy making process, and shake public confidence in the conclusions of climate science.

The Greening Earth Society is one portal from which to view these efforts. Quite understandably, you might think that The Greening Earth Society is an environmentally-oriented group. But you would be wrong. The Greening Earth Society is a creation of the Western Fuels Association, a $400 million coal producer co-op.

From its website, www.greeningearthsociety.org, this benevolent-sounding "green organization" serves as a gateway to coal, oil, and mining industry-funded think tanks and institutes as well as to publications rife with misinformation. Some of the materials circulated by the "Just Say 'No' to Climate Change" folks even target elementary school children through their teachers.

Climate skeptics also play a critical role in the coal and oil industry's efforts to foster doubts about climate science and fears of an economic meltdown. Although they present themselves to the public as independent scientists or respected climate experts, most of the best known of these "objective thinkers" have taken significant amounts of energy industry money for themselves or their organizations and espouse scientifically dubious positions.

Prominent examples include Dr. S. Fred Singer, funded by Exxon, Shell, Unocal, ARCO, and Sun Oil; Dr. Pat Michaels, recipient of at least $165,000 from coal and other energy interests; Dr. Richard Lindzen of MIT, who has received money from the Western Fuels Association; and climatologist Dr. Robert Balling of Arizona State University, whose work has received over $300,000 from coal and oil interests.[1]

Individuals like these, espousing views far outside mainstream climate science, have paraded before the media, their presence falsely suggesting a pervasive schism among climate scientists and obscuring the wide consensus that exists. At times some of them have merely recycled already discredited scientific opinion in the belief that the public would be unable to sort out the truth.

In doing so, they enjoyed a great advantage. It is usually much easier to make wild charges than to disprove them. Unwary or irresponsible members of the press have often given these views equal time with those of responsible, reputable climate scientists, thereby creating the false impression that the basic ideas of climate science are in dispute. Uninformed readers and listeners might then be inclined to regard both sides of the make-believe controversy as equally credible, and "split the difference," since one side said there was a serious problem and the other side claimed there was none.

For an example of just how irresponsible a newspaper can be in publishing nonsense about climate change, see, "Science Has Spoken: Global Warming Is a Myth," which appeared in *The Wall Street Journal* on December 4, 1997. Its authors, chemist Arthur Robinson and his son Zachary, run the tiny "Oregon Institute of Science and Medicine," outside Cave Junction, Oregon, from which they market nuclear bomb shelters and home-schooling advice.

Relying on the erroneous claim that changes in solar activity explain the Earth's increase in temperature since the Little Ice Age, the article concludes, "There is not a shred of persuasive evidence that humans have been responsible for increasing global temperatures." The article then soothingly advises readers not to worry "about human use of hydrocarbons warming the Earth."

"Carbon dioxide emissions have actually been a boon for the environment," the article states. "Our children will enjoy an Earth with twice as much plant and animal life as that with which we are now blessed. This is a wonderful and unexpected gift from the industrial revolution."

Another attempt to cloak the climate disinformation campaign in the mantle of science was a "Global Warming Petition" supposedly signed by "17,000 U.S. scientists," but whose names were published without any identifying titles or affiliations. (The list included author John Grisham, several actors from the TV series M*A*S*H*, and a Spice Girl.) The petition was circulated by none other than Dr. Robinson's Oregon Institute of Science and Medicine.[2]

With the petition came a bogus "eight-page abstract of the latest research on climate change," formatted to look like a published scientific article from the prestigious *Proceedings of the National Academy of Sciences*, with which it had no connection.

Filled with misinformation and put together by the Robinsons and two coauthors affiliated with The George C. Marshall Institute, the tract was accompanied by a letter of endorsement from Dr. Frederick Seitz, a former president of the National Academy of Sciences in the 1960s, who contends that "global warming is a myth." Dr. Seitz is not a climatologist and in the opinion of at least two very prominent scientists, "has no expertise in climate matters." He is, however, "one of the last remaining scientists who insist that humans have not altered the stratospheric ozone layer, despite an over-whelming body of evidence to the contrary."[3]

A Chorus of Climate Skeptics

Contemporary tactics in the coal and oil industries' challenge to cli-mate science can be traced back at least to the formation of the In-formation Council on the Environment (ICE) in 1991, formed by The National Coal Association, the Western Fuels Association, the Edison Electric Institute, and others.[4]

Bracy Williams & Co., a Washington, D.C. PR firm, was hired to run the organization with a $500,000 budget for advertising and public relations. They assembled a "scientific advisory panel" con-sisting of climate skeptics to further ICE's self-described mission: to "reposition global warming as theory (not fact)." But thanks to the leak of internal memos, the ICE campaign was aborted.[5]

The demise of one industry-funded front organization, how-ever, did little to deter the fossil fuel industry from pursing its long-term goal of stalemating action on climate change. They merely ad-vanced their agenda through other channels.

Perhaps the most important of these is The Global Climate Coalition, set up by the PR firm of Burson-Marsteller for the fossil fuel industry and its allies in 1989. Meeting at the offices of the Na-tional Association of Manufacturers, this influential coalition has been the apparent hub of the fossil fuel industry's climate campaign. From 1994 at least through 1998, the GCC spent upwards of $1 mil-lion a year to promote its climate views.

GCC members include The Aluminum Association, The Ameri-can Forest and Paper Association, the American Petroleum Insti-tute, ARCO, Chevron, Cyprus AMAX Minerals, the Edison Electric Institute, Exxon, Mobil, Goodyear Tire and Rubber, The Southern Company, Texaco, railroads, and some 40 other companies. (Former members BP-Amoco, Shell, Chrysler, Dow Chemical, General Motors, and Ford have recently abandoned the coalition.)

Additional PR services were bought from E. Bruce Harrison Co. Mr. Harrison is known for leading the pesticide industry's attack on author Rachel Carson and her widely praised book *Silent Spring* in the 1960s, which sounded a loud and overdue alarm about the environmental harm caused by pesticides.[6]

Another important communications arm of the oil and coal industries is The Global Climate Information Project, founded in 1997 and guided by Shandwick Public Affairs, a Washington, D.C. PR firm which had a $13 million war chest for its climate change advertising campaign. The Project promptly spent more than $3 million on ads designed to instill public fears that the Kyoto Protocol would add a half-dollar tax to the price of gasoline while raising prices on everything else.[7]

The large automobile manufacturers used similar tactics through their Coalition for Vehicle Choice (CVC), which paid for an expensive ad campaign to reinforce the idea that the Kyoto accord would hobble the U.S. economy.

Several other industry-funded groups have been active in disseminating industry allegations:[8]

- **The Cato Institute**, a libertarian think tank supported by oil and chemical industry dollars and conservative foundations, serves as a base for Dr. Patrick Michaels, a prominent climate skeptic.
- **Consumer Alert**, funded by big oil and chemical corporations among others, operates a coalition of twenty-four nonprofits known as the National Consumer Coalition (NCC). A "Cooler Heads Coalition" within the NCC serves as the group's voice on climate issues.
- **The Competitive Enterprise Institute**, which supports the anti-environmental "Wise Use" movement, set in motion a series of anti-Kyoto conferences. "The Costs of Kyoto," its

first, provided a platform for attacks on climate science and for predictions that Kyoto would be an economic disaster.

- **The Environmental Conservation Organization**, another bastion of the "Wise Use" movement, espouses conspiracy theories featuring the United Nations and environmentalists' designs to create a "one-world government."

- **The Frontiers of Freedom Institute** opposes environmental regulations, such as the Endangered Species Act, and co-sponsored "Countdown to Kyoto," an anti-Kyoto conference in Australia that showcased prominent climate skeptics.

- **The George C. Marshall Institute**, another libertarian think-tank, is closely identified with the anti-climate change lobby and is funded by right-wing foundations. Its chairman, Dr. Frederick Seitz, has acknowledged that the Institute does not do original climate research and that its reports are fundamentally expressions of opinion.[9]

- **People for the American West!**, funded by mining interests, portrays itself as a grassroots group while it lobbies for mining, timber, and other industries that exploit public lands.

- **The Science and Environmental Policy Project** is run by climate skeptic Dr. S. Fred Singer, a former ozone-hole doubter who has taken consulting fees from at least half a dozen major oil companies as well as from cigarette and chemical firms.

A More Reasonable Approach

Not all fossil fuel producers, nor all large corporate fossil fuel consumers, have chosen to cast their lots in with the Global Climate Coalition and its questionable friends. Various large oil, gas, chemical, and utility companies have joined the Business Environmental Leadership Council (BELC) of the Pew Center on Global Climate Change, distancing themselves from fellow industry members who categorically oppose carbon emission reductions.

BELC members include American Electric Power Company, BP-Amoco, CH2M-Hill, Dupont, Enron, Shell International, Sunoco, and Toyota. These companies have played a leadership role in adopting positions on climate change that were not initially popular in their industries.

BELC accepts the views of most scientists that enough is known about climate change to take action. It advocates emission reductions by business through improved energy efficiency, and it recognizes the Kyoto agreement as an important first step toward further international cooperation.

Some of the companies in this camp have made important investments in energy efficiency and a few—BP-Amoco and Shell— have invested significantly in clean energy technologies as well, although those commitments are small relative to the size of the companies' fossil fuel businesses. To their credit, BP-Amoco, Shell, and Elf Aquitaine have committed themselves to reducing their own emissions below the targets of the Kyoto Protocol, and both BP and Shell have publicly acknowledged that an eventual shift to noncarbon fuels is inevitable.

These companies appear prepared to accept a slow global movement toward clean energy technologies (and are positioning themselves to profit from it) so long as it is gradual enough not to jeopardize their fossil fuel revenues. Whereas the stand of the BELC firms took foresight and courage, it leaves them far from a vanguard position on how urgently the world should pursue a transition to clean energy. The BELC companies mainly support neoliberal market mechanisms for solving climate problems, including heavy reliance on emissions trading and voluntary emissions reductions.

The Business Council for a Sustainable Energy Future is another business coalition that supports moderate actions to stem climate change. Members include companies engaged in renewable energy, energy efficiency, natural gas, and a few electric utilities. The natural gas industry thrives on concern about carbon dioxide and sees it as a way of taking market share from the coal industry.

Whereas the moderates in the business community are not as likely to stand in the way of measures to combat climate change, they are also unlikely to be the driving force that produces a timely solution.

Climate Myths

Now, let's analyze the principal myths that the hard line oil and chemical interests have used to build their case.

Myth One:
The scientific foundation for concerns about climate change is uncertain and unproven. The evidence is contradictory and inconclusive.

Response:
After years of research—and the preparation of hundreds of meticulously peer-reviewed studies—some 2,500 of the world's leading scientists with knowledge of climate issues concluded in 1995 that, "The balance of evidence suggests a discernible human influence on global climate."

Their comprehensive and evenhanded series of reports, *Climate Change 1995*, has become the standard reference for policy-makers, scientists, and all serious students of climate issues.[10]

Collaborating in a multidisciplinary alliance known as the Intergovernmental Panel on Climate Change (IPCC) under the auspices of the UN and the World Meteorological Organization, these eminent scientists reached profound agreement on the causes of climate change and its probable impacts. Their forecasts integrate a prodigious body of long-term physical data gathered from all over the world by experts in many scientific disciplines.

Despite this broad scientific agreement, and the millions of hours of labor invested in attaining it, the scientists involved prominently identified a number of uncertainties in their findings. The uncertainties pertain to the exact rate of climate change expected, the magnitude of its impacts and their regional effects.

Given the tremendous complexity of the systems being studied, it is hardly surprising that precise answers are not yet available to all these questions. Whereas these uncertainties cannot be dismissed as trivial, they are of far less importance than the over-arching conclusion that human actions are disrupting the climate and that, if the disruptive behavior is not corrected, the world will inevitably suffer a worsening series of tragic consequences.

Climate scientists may have inadvertently fostered the notion that the uncertainties remaining are more significant and fundamental than they really are because true scientists tend to take their areas of agreement for granted and focus on their remaining differences, however minor, in the spirit of discovering the truth.[11]

"We don't know everything about this subject but we know a lot," says Professor John P. Holdren of Harvard University. "And what we know suggests that the downside risks of failing to deal with it are very large."[12]

So should we wait until all uncertainties are resolved and all answers are in? Stanford Professor Stephen Schneider disagrees. "Science," he says, "is never 100 percent certain of anything." To hold action hostage to a standard of 100 percent certainty would be absurd and, in this case, dangerous.

Myth Two:
Climate varies naturally. We are in a natural warming cycle that has little or nothing to do with human influence.

Response:
Over the past century, the world's temperature rose about 1°F—*ten times faster* than the rate of temperature increase that is characteris-

tic of warming periods over past millennia. That strongly suggests that the climate change underway is not natural.

In addition, the recent rise in global temperatures bears an indelible "human fingerprint." Climate scientists have identified a complex, predictable pattern that accompanies atmospheric warming caused by human action. This phenomenon, which involves cooling of the upper atmosphere and warming of the lower atmosphere, is characteristic of the global temperature changes now observed. The probability that natural fluctuations could reproduce these consistent patterns by chance, without human intervention, is extremely low.

Skeptics also claim that natural variations in solar radiation are responsible for changes in global temperature. But studies based on sophisticated analysis of several centuries of temperature data show that the changes in solar energy could account for no more than a tenth of the global warming observed over the past century.[13] Furthermore, climate models indicate that astronomical factors, such as changes in the Earth's orbit or the Earth's tilt, are likely to be responsible for a gradual *cooling* of the Earth, starting 6,000 years ago. The warming of the past 100 years, therefore, is especially *un*natural in that it interrupted, and then very dramatically reversed, a prolonged natural cooling cycle.

Myth Three:
The world is really cooling, not warming.

Response:
The proposition is that somehow the entire community of scientific climate experts has been blind-sided on the basic direction of global temperature change.

The climate skeptics making this argument have long ago run out of legitimate objections to climate science and therefore have relied on claims like:

- Global temperature readings are upwardly biased because they come from weather stations in or around cities where the "heat island" effect has distorted temperature readings.
- Temperature measurements were made on land but not over cooler ocean surfaces.
- Even if surface temperatures may have gone up, satellite data prove that the Earth is cooling.

The first two objections are simply false. Urban temperature data have been carefully corrected for urban heat island effects, and ample temperature measurements have been taken at sea. A distinct upward temperature trend is evident in all this data.[14]

Regarding satellite data, it is true that satellite measurements of temperatures at altitudes of 5,000-30,000 feet indicate global warming at less than the rate forecast by some climate models. However, they do not refute the fact that the Earth is warming. First, readings taken over a larger layer of the atmosphere from the same satellite data are significantly warmer. Second, the use of satellites for temperature measurements is a relatively new development. To extract long-term trends will require a longer historical record.[15]

By contrast, the finding that the Earth is warming rests on more than a century and a half of surface temperature measurements, and on the historic climate record obtained from natural indicators going back about 420,000 years.

Myth Four:
There's no cause for alarm. The warming observed is gradual and slight. The dire projections of climate change impacts are vastly exaggerated.

Response:
The scientific community projects a 1.8-6.3°F temperature increase over the next century. Although this may seem like a small increase, it is enough to change the incidence of extreme high and low tem-

peratures (which affects plant and insect life cycles), alter the timing of seasons, raise sea level, and modify precipitation patterns.

Remember that average surface Ice Age temperatures were only 9°F colder than at present. A few degrees can make a huge difference.

A shift in global average temperature of several degrees over a century is not gradual—indeed it is very fast. The change into and out of Ice Ages has typically occurred far more slowly.[16] Because of the swiftness of contemporary warming, many ecosystems will be unable to adapt and will perish or be severely stressed.

In addition, whereas global average temperature may change 1.8-6.3°F, regional changes may be larger. The higher latitudes of the Northern Hemisphere will warm very substantially more than the global average. So, too, will the interior of continents.

Myth Five:
Climate change takes place slowly and is therefore a long-term problem that merits a long-term solution, not a quick fix. We should wait and see what happens.

Response:
Time is of the essence in keeping heat-trapping gas emissions from getting perilously higher. According to the International Energy Agency, if we do nothing to counteract current energy use trends, the global carbon emissions rate will be fifty percent higher in 2010 than in 1990. Acting promptly to lower emissions rates will reduce risk and accelerate the arrival of important benefits.

It is not enough to merely halt the increase of global carbon emissions. Even if we hold current emissions steady, carbon dioxide and other gases will still accumulate in the atmosphere faster than natural processes can remove them. Scientists have calculated that greenhouse gas emissions must ultimately be reduced by a factor of three or four to bring global concentrations back to safe levels.

There is also little reason to assume that just because energy technology will advance, the reduction of emissions will be easier for our children twenty years from now than today. Unless we alter our habits now, our children will have to make drastically deeper cuts than we would. And by then, a needlessly inflated stock of expensive, fossil fuel energy infrastructure will have to be converted to noncarbon energy sources.

New power plants typically have a 20-40 year operating life. Permitting the construction of new coal- and natural gas-powered generating plants today commits the world to polluting technology for decades and will confront people ten or twenty years from now with the dilemma of shutting down working power plants before the end of their useful lives or facing high-carbon emissions for additional decades.

Myth Six:
Global warming is a blessing in disguise. In fact, it is good for us.

Response:
This is the ultimate contrarian argument. It goes like this. Plants will benefit from increased carbon dioxide levels—after all, carbon dioxide is a nutrient—and with fewer frosts and a longer growing season, agriculture as a whole will benefit. Fish will grow faster and bigger in a warmer world. And people will benefit as there will be fewer cold winters and fewer deaths from hypothermia. Transportation and communication costs will fall.[17]

These are very simplistic arguments that do not stand up to scrutiny. Climate change *will* have some positive impacts for some people. In northern latitudes, growing seasons will lengthen, new areas will be suitable for cropping, home heating bills may fall, and people may have to spend less for snow removal. The ice-free shipping season will lengthen in the Arctic and on waterways such as the Great Lakes and the Saint Lawrence seaway.

On balance, however, these modest benefits do not begin to

compensate for the far more devastating socioeconomic and environmental impacts that climate change will have. Soil instability from melting permafrost in the north will counterbalance some of the northern-latitude benefits just mentioned. As for agriculture, hoped-for increases in crop yields in northern latitudes will be tempered by the unknown impacts of warmer temperatures on pests, pathogens, and weeds, and by agricultural losses elsewhere.

As pointed out in earlier chapters, human health will suffer greatly from the spread of diseases, more frequent heat waves, exacerbated air pollution, and weather-related catastrophes. Thus, the profoundly negative effects of climate change far outweigh the minor reduction in cold-related health effects.

Myth Seven:
Combating climate change would be so expensive that we should wait for more evidence before taking action. Countermeasures would raise energy prices, raise taxes, lower household incomes, reduce business investment, devastate key industries, and cost the economy jobs.

Response:
These claims are groundless or grossly exaggerated scare tactics that rest on the "authority" of oil-industry funded studies. Nonindustry studies have come to completely different conclusions.[18]

One U.S. Department of Energy study found that carbon emissions could be reduced to 1990 levels by 2010 at roughly *zero net costs*. The DOE study did not even include the environmental and public health benefits that would accrue to the economy from trimming U.S. energy waste and phasing in some low-carbon electricity supply technologies.

Far from requiring prohibitively expensive carbon taxes, the researchers found that the U.S. could return to its 1990 emission levels merely by implementing a system of tradable emission permits valued at $50 per ton of carbon emitted. Another research effort con-

Emissions Trading

Emissions trading is a market-based process for reducing the release of pollutants into the environment. Here is how it works:

At the start of a trading period, participants are assigned an emissions quota or permit by a designated authority. A trading participant may then either use the allowance, releasing the authorized emissions, or the party may sell the allowance. The issuance of emission permits thus creates a market in emissions and allows participants to trade to their advantage.

An entity whose emissions are high and which lacks a necessary allowance will either have to purchase an unused emissions permit from another party or adopt emission-avoidance technology, whichever is cheaper.

The Kyoto Protocol (see page 43) authorizes its parties to trade portions of heat-trapping gas emission allowances. In the U.S., domestic emissions trading has worked outstandingly well in reducing industrial sulfur dioxide emissions—and at far lower cost than industrial polluters had projected.

ducted by the Department of Energy and the EPA, aided by the Departments of Commerce, Treasury, Labor, and State, found that losses in economic output stemming from even a $100 per ton carbon emission permit system would be small and transient. No evidence was found that the emissions reduction policy would provoke a flight of capital from the U.S.

A third study led by the nonprofit Tellus Institute also examined the costs of reducing carbon emissions. The Institute found that energy use by 2010 could realistically be reduced by fifteen percent, and that carbon emissions would then fall by almost ten percent below 1990 levels. Instead of imposing unacceptable costs on the economy, this process would lead to the creation of 800,000 new jobs; the average household would realize energy savings of $530 per year; the gross national product would increase slightly relative to business as usual; and wage and salary incomes would rise by $14 billion. Tellus forecast that by 2030, greater energy efficiency could reduce U.S. energy consumption by more than forty percent without any loss of services or comfort .

Where then do the claims of damage to the economy come from? One source is a recent, widely-quoted study sponsored by the Global Climate Coalition and funded by the American Petroleum Institute. It contains preposterous estimates for the economic damage that would be caused by U.S. adherence to the Kyoto Protocol, including predictions of sharp increases in gasoline prices—a charge that always touches a nerve for the motoring public.[19]

Based on the outrageous assumption that a huge tax of $241 per ton of carbon would have to be imposed to meet the Kyoto targets, this analysis reached the outlandish conclusion that implementing the Kyoto Protocol would force energy and electricity prices to double, costing the U.S. economy 2.4 million jobs and $300 billion a year. Each household allegedly would suffer a $2,728 loss in gross domestic product by 2010.

Typically, studies like this ignore virtually all costs of not reducing emissions, as well as indirect benefits of reducing them, such as lower heath care costs, trade and export expansion, domestic job creation, and gains in worker productivity.

Myth Eight:
Protecting the climate puts an unfair burden on the developed nations to reduce their greenhouse gas emissions without obligating developing nations to do their part.

Response:

Current carbon emissions from the highly industrialized nations are far greater than those from the developing ones—almost twice as great when land use and industrial sources are considered. The U.S. alone produces a quarter of the world's carbon emissions.[20]

The developed nations' carbon additions are even greater on a *per capita* basis, since the population of the developing nations is four times the size of the developed world. For example, every year the U.S. releases more than five and a half tons of carbon per person from fossil fuel. By contrast, India's industrial emissions are roughly 700 pounds per person, and 120 other nations each produce less than 2,200 pounds per person.[21]

It is therefore neither unfair nor inappropriate for the developed nations to initiate the process of reducing the world's greenhouse gas emissions. The wealthier nations are not only more responsible for the buildup of atmospheric carbon, but they have benefited more from creating it, and are far better able to afford emission-reducing investments.

Because China and India and other developing nations are rapidly increasing their industrial carbon emissions, they will have to accept emissions limitations eventually. But until developed nations begin meeting their own responsibilities and commitments to protect the climate, many developing nations will feel justified in ignoring the problem.

Myth Nine:
Adherence to international climate agreements amounts to forfeiting national sovereignty to unelected global authorities. They leave the developed nations hostage to the whims of the developing world.

Response:
These arguments over national sovereignty are espoused by those who are willing to partake in the economic benefits of globalization

but not in its responsibilities. The entire world shares the same atmosphere. Chinese, Russian, American, Indonesian, and French carbon dioxide are all commingled as the atmosphere mixes and winds circle the globe. The buildup of carbon in the atmosphere obviously requires international cooperation.

By engaging in negotiations, we do not forfeit national sovereignty. To the contrary, acting as a sovereign nation, we make beneficial agreements with others that protect our common interests in a healthy climate. To the extent that we choose to accept limits on the discharge of heat-trapping gases, we do so intentionally to accomplish a greater good.

Decisions under the Kyoto Protocol, which was signed voluntarily, are made by consensus. No one is forced to comply. The one-nation, one-vote decision process certainly does not mean that large powerful nations like the U.S. do not have far more clout than small, less industrialized nations.

If the U.S. tenaciously advocates a position, it is likely to sway other nations and get its way. If its position is not adopted, the U.S. has the option of declining to agree and thereby of blocking consensus on that point. By contrast, if a tiny developing nation objects to a proposal, it is far less likely to convince other signatories to adopt its position, and it may have little recourse but to agree or withdraw.

The charge that the Kyoto agreement places the U.S. and other nations under the governance of unelected global authorities is equally misguided. In a democracy, governments routinely delegate authority to negotiators to draft international agreements. Moreover, the Vice-President of the United States played a significant role in the Kyoto negotiations, and the President strongly endorses it. Support for the agreement is strong in other democracies, and in the U.S., a 1999 poll found that eighty-four percent of the public believes it is important for the U.S. to take action now to reduce emissions of heat-trapping gases.

Undeterred by Facts, The Campaign Continues

Whereas a decade ago the oil and coal industries and their allies could get away with denying global warming and with attacking the notion that humanity was changing the climate, by the late 1990s, that strategy was no longer viable.

The oil and coal industry and their supporters have nonetheless continued repeating their old claims, while updating their campaign with more subtle allegations.

The latest contention *du jour* (and it will be different tomorrow) is that, although climate change may be real, and may not even be so good for the world after all, the most prudent, cost-effective response is to study the problem and defer action to a future date. Whenever that date arrives, the energy industry and its allies can then always call for more research and set a new date for action even farther away in the future.

Until people lose patience with this stalling and the deceptive campaigning that goes with it, industries that benefit from fossil fuels will keep fabricating new climate theories, and the Earth's climate will remain at risk.

People in the U.S. and other technologically advanced nations must mobilize enough political support to tackle emissions reduction over industries' objections. Otherwise, real solutions to climate change will remain impossible.

In chapter five, we will outline these solutions, and in chapter six, we will present the means for implementing them.

CHAPTER FIVE

Climate-Safe Energy Sources

Imagine if—instead of getting ninety-five percent of our energy supplies in the U.S. from fossil fuels and nuclear power as we do now—we created a truly safe, clean energy future.

Air pollution would plummet. Skies would clear. Water pollution from fuel spills, mining, and transportation would be reduced to a trickle. Acid rain would disappear. Lakes and streams would sparkle. Nuclear power plant accident risks would wane. Nuclear waste production would taper off. The threat of global climate change due to human activities would vanish.

The U.S. would go from being the world's major cause of global warming to being the world's premier source of clean energy systems. Millions of new jobs would be created, along with billions of dollars of new economic activity. At the same time, trillions of dollars in fossil fuel costs and devastating environmental and public health impacts would be avoided.[1]

Although this future may sound unattainable, it isn't. The U.S. and the world have the technology today to cleanly meet their energy needs.

What Is and Isn't Renewable?

Solar, hydropower, geothermal, and wind resources all provide high quality energy without carbon emissions. They are called "renewable" resources because they are endlessly replenished by nature.

By contrast, fossil fuels, such as coal, petroleum, and natural gas, were created over millions of years; exist in limited quantities; and are nonrenewable. We consume them, and the more we use, the less remains. Because economically exploitable deposits of these carbon fuels will one day be exhausted, a sustainable energy economy must rely on renewable energy sources.

Why not include nuclear power on this menu?

- Nuclear power fuel is made from uranium ores which are in limited supply and nonrenewable. To produce nuclear power indefinitely, uranium eventually would have to be replaced with highly radioactive, reprocessed plutonium, creating serious safety, proliferation, and economic problems.
- Nuclear power generation presents safety and environmental hazards. They range from routine radioactive emissions from power plants to catastrophic accident risks due to power plant malfunctions, earthquakes or terrorism, as well as dangers arising from nuclear materials transport and storage.
- Nuclear power plants are exceptionally costly to build, maintain, and decommission.
- The nuclear fuel cycle involves uranium mining, milling, and fuel fabrication, all of which use energy from fossil fuel, and generate radioactive waste.[2]

The Role of Renewables

Renewables are already playing a large part in the energy supply of other nations. Iceland and Norway get almost 100 percent of their electricity from renewable energy sources—mainly hydropower. Iceland also gets almost 100 percent of its heat from renewable sources—mainly from geothermal energy. Denmark will get fifty percent of its electricity from wind power by 2030. New Zealand gets about three-quarters of its electricity from hydro and geothermal sources. The U.S. itself, in the 1940s, got forty percent of its electricity from hydroelectric facilities.[3]

Naturally, the spectrum of affordable renewable energy sources

Table 1: Where the Energy We Used Came From in 1997[4]

Source	U.S. (%)	World (%)
Oil	38.0	34.0
Coal	24.0	24.0
Natural Gas	25.0	20.0
Biomass Fuels	3.8	13.0
Nuclear	7.7	6.4
Hydroelectric	1.3	2.3
Solar/Wind/Geothermal	0.2	0.3

today is far broader than just hydro and geothermal power, and the U.S. has much more generous natural renewable energy resource endowments than the Nordic nations or New Zealand. As Table 3 shows (page 97), the U.S. could easily develop a clean energy economy in thirty years. Let's have a look now at some of the energy sources that can make this possible.

Power From the Wind is a Breeze

Wind is an economical, pollution-free, inexhaustible domestic energy resource. Picture a tower 160 feet tall with three blades extending eighty feet outward from an aerodynamically sculpted hub. As strong winds spin the blades, an alternator mounted behind the rotor produces a million watts (1 MW) of clean electricity. No gaseous emissions, no particulates, no wastewater, no solid waste. And wind turbines can be used singly, in small clusters, or in big wind farms connected to large power supply grids.

Thanks to steeply falling costs and rapidly advancing technology, wind capacity is growing faster than any other energy technology in the world. In the 1990s, wind power capacity tripled every three years.[5] By the end of 1998, world wind capacity was 9,600 MW, and worldwide investment in wind power was roughly $11 billion.

Further expansions of wind capacity are under development in nearly forty countries.

If appropriate policies are adopted, wind could produce ten percent of the world's electricity by 2020. BTM Consult, the international wind energy consulting firm, calculated that 1.2 million MW of wind capacity could be installed in the next two decades. That would produce as much electricity as Europe now consumes while creating 1.7 million new jobs and avoiding billions of tons of carbon dioxide emissions. Just with current trends and policies, Europe's wind capacity will rise to 100,000 MW by 2020.

U.S. wind capacity—now around 2,500 MW—is expected to more than triple by 2010. All regions except the Southeast have wind resources that can be commercially developed with current technology. Commercial wind turbines already operate in California, Texas, Hawaii, Minnesota, and Vermont.

The Department of Energy has set a wind capacity target of 80,000 MW by 2020 for the U.S., but no technological reason prevents the U.S. from achieving wind energy targets at least as ambitious as those of Europe. If the U.S. were to install 100,000 MW of wind power in the next two decades, it would produce enough power to supply 27 million American homes, and reduce U.S. carbon emissions by 200 million tons.

Even if these goals are achieved, prodigious untapped wind resources will still remain in North America, Central Asia, Europe, and Latin America. The U.S. easily has sufficient wind resources to produce three times the nation's 1990 power consumption.

Our huge wind resources are an energy bonanza. At the average residential electricity price of about 6.8 cents per kilowatt-hour today, our wind resources could generate revenues of more than $140 billion dollars a year for U.S. producers.

Wind only provides intermittent power unless an energy storage system is added at an additional cost. Yet wind is quite predictable on a regional basis. Even in the absence of energy storage, wind

Table 2: Renewable Energy Resources and the Services They Provide

Resource	Energy Service
Biomass	Electricity
	Gaseous fuels for heat, power, and transportation
	Liquid fuels, primarily for transportation
	Solid fuels for combined heat and power
Geothermal	Combined heat and power
	Electricity
	Heat
Hydropower	Electricity
	Mechanical power
	Electricity storage
Solar Energy	Electricity
	Lighting
	Process heat
	Space conditioning (heating and cooling)
	Waste detoxification
	Water heating
Wind	Electricity
	Mechanical power

power could provide twenty percent or more of U.S. electricity needs without undermining power grid reliability. That share rises to thirty percent if low-cost natural gas turbine power plants are used to compensate for wind fluctuations.

Wind Power: Ever-Cheaper
Wind power costs vary from site to site with the quality of the wind resource and the cost of project financing. Utility-scale wind projects

at the best sites can produce wind power at about 3.5-5 cents a kilowatt-hour. At the lower end of this price range, wind is very competitive with power from some coal and natural gas plants. By 2030, wind power costs in constant 1998 dollars should be only 2.5-3 cents per kilowatt-hour for taxpaying corporations and, in excellent wind areas, at the astoundingly low price of 1.5 cents per kilowatt-hour for municipal utilities, which pay no income or property taxes.

Water Power

In times past, water power turned grindstones and was harnessed by leather belts to sawmill blades. Today, mention hydropower and people think of Hoover or Grand Coulee Dams. The sizable contribution of hydroelectricity to our power supplies these days belies the common notion that renewables are all new and experimental additions to the power grid.

Hydro facilities are the cheapest to operate of all conventional power plants. Their disadvantages are their high construction costs, and their many environmental and human impacts.

The nation has about 80,000 MW of installed hydroelectric generating capacity—almost ten percent of total U.S. electric capacity—and nineteen percent of the world's electricity came from hydropower in 1997. Water power currently provides more than seven times the electrical capacity of biomass, the nation's next largest source of renewably generated electricity.

But hydro faces limits to its growth. It is a mature commercial technology, and most of the major hydro sites have already been developed in the U.S. Those that remain are typically constrained from development for economic, regulatory, and environmental reasons. Little additional new large hydro construction is expected.

Existing hydro capacity can be significantly expanded, however, without new dam construction. Some 20,000 MW of undeveloped hydro capacity existed at U.S. dams in 1997. Upgrading dams, by adding new turbines or rewinding old ones, could thus increase hydroelectric power generation by twenty-five percent, at relatively little cost, and it also might present opportunities for improving fish passage, downstream aquatic habitats, and water quality.

Energy from the Sun

Solar Heating

When captured by suitable mechanical and electrical devices, the Sun's energy can meet significant portions of the space-conditioning and hot water needs of buildings—typically 30-70 percent in residences. It can also be concentrated to provide process heat for industry, water purification, detoxification of hazardous wastes, and heat for cooking.

Some 1.3 million U.S. buildings now use solar water heating. A quarter million commercial, industrial, and institutional buildings—including schools, military bases, offices, and prisons—use solar energy to heat space or water, or both. Solar water heaters can provide 40-80 percent of an ordinary household's hot water demands, depending on the climate.

Solar Cooling

Like solar heating equipment, solar-powered cooling systems use solar energy gathered in various types of heat collectors. Instead of pumping heat into the house, they heat a pressurized refrigerant and cause it to evaporate in order to cool the surrounding air. Such evaporative cooling systems can typically provide 30-60 percent of a building's cooling requirements, and this technology is being actively pushed toward commercialization by the DOE.[6]

Passive Solar Energy

Passive solar buildings are designed to reduce heating and cooling needs by strategically using sunlight, shade, and thermal building materials. Many beautiful modern buildings today use passive solar features, like skylights and interior courts. More than 250,000 homes in the U.S. now have at least some deliberately-designed passive solar features. The use of solar energy in these buildings is more cost-effective than active solar heating and cooling systems would be.

People have known for decades that when passive solar features are coupled with appropriate insulation and advanced windows in a holistic building design effort, vast reductions in building energy use are possible. A 1981 study by the Federal Solar Energy Research Institute concluded that, "New residential and commercial buildings can be built to use about a quarter of the energy . . . for heating and cooling required by the typical unit built in the U.S. today."[7]

Biomass Energy

Biomass has been a popular energy source ever since our ancestors huddled in caves around wood fires. The term literally means living matter, and is used to refer to any organic material derived from plant or animal tissue. Its use adds no net carbon to the atmosphere since the carbon released when biomass burns was earlier extracted by plants *from* the atmosphere.

Biomass resources that can be converted to usable energy are abundant and diverse. They include residues from sugar and paper production, agriculture and forestry, as well as municipal solid wastes and crops grown specifically for energy purposes. An extremely versatile resource, biomass can be converted to solid, liquid, and gaseous ("biogas") fuels.

Livestock manure and other organic waste, for example, can be "biodigested" by microorganisms to form methane, the main ingredient in natural gas. This biologically-produced methane can then be burned for process heat or power generation, or compressed and upgraded for distribution through natural gas pipelines or for conversion to electricity in fuel cells. Capturing and using methane is infinitely preferable to allowing the release of this heat-trapping gas during natural waste decomposition.

Biomass can also be converted to ethanol and methanol, liquid fuels that add no net carbon dioxide to the air. Forestry wastes and biomass grown on idle farmland could produce 240 billion gallons of ethanol annually, which would replace 160 billion gallons of gasoline. If U.S. biomass resources were converted instead to methanol, they could displace more than 268 billion gallons. Since the U.S. uses only about 121 billion gallons of gasoline each year, biomass fuels could more than meet the fuel needs of cars and other light duty vehicles, according to the National Renewable Energy Laboratory.

While biomass grown especially for energy is not economically competitive with fossil fuels today in the U.S., the Intergovernmental Panel on Climate Change found that "biomass has good prospects for competition with coal by 2020 in many circumstances, even if the price of biomass is somewhat higher than the price of coal."[8] Several U.S. utilities are already burning biomass together with coal, reducing carbon dioxide and other harmful emissions.

Within two or three decades, it is projected that biomass energy crops could provide the U.S. with 100,000 MW of electrical generating capacity—twelve percent of 1998 U.S. capacity. Raising the crops would take just 50 million acres. For comparison, the U.S. now plants 72 million acres in soybeans, and 128 million acres of cropland are projected to be idle in 2030.

Hydrogen Fuel and Fuel Cells

You can't see it or smell it. It's the lightest element on the Periodic Table. It's the source of the Sun's heat and the most common element in the universe. It's also a key to tomorrow's clean-energy future. The element is hydrogen, a high-quality, easy-to-use energy source that can produce electricity, heat, or synthetic chemicals. Cars, buses, and trucks fueled with hydrogen can be virtually pollution-free.

Fuel cells, which combine hydrogen and oxygen to produce heat and electricity, are quiet, high efficiency, modular devices. They can be fueled by pure hydrogen, natural gas, or other hydrocarbon fuels, and are commercially available in large sizes for stationary power production. A few fuel cell vehicles are on the road today. Daimler-Chrysler has developed one prototype, the NECAR 4, that reaches ninety miles per hour and can go 280 miles on a single fueling.

As their costs fall through technical advances and mass production, hydrogen fuel cells will eventually become competitive for use in homes for on-site power generation, space conditioning, and water heating.

Currently, the most economical way to produce hydrogen is by reacting natural gas with steam. That, however, continues our dependence on fossil fuel. Hydrogen can be produced more cleanly, although at greater cost, from ordinary water by electrolysis—the splitting of H_2O into hydrogen and oxygen by electric current. If the electricity comes from carbon-free sources, no heat-trapping gases are released. Hydrogen could also be produced without any net carbon emissions from biomass, or relatively cleanly from gasified coal in plants equipped to capture and store carbon dioxide.

Capturing carbon in the coal-burning process is not yet commercial, but ultimately is projected to add relatively little to overall coal gasification costs. If it can be done cheaply and safely enough, carbon capture will allow coal to play a prominent role in the world's energy future, not as a raw fuel for direct combustion processes, but as a source of clean-burning, hydrogen-rich fuels.

Electric and Hybrid Vehicles

Electric cars are so silent and vibration-free that when you turn the key, you don't even know they're running unless you look at the instrument panel. Like fuel cell vehicles, these battery electric vehicles (EVs) are extremely efficient, as well as clean, quiet, easy to maintain, and economical to operate. Tailpipe emissions are zero, and, if charged with electricity from renewable resources, the entire fuel cycle is carbon-free or carbon neutral.

Hybrid electrics, which use a small, fuel-burning engine along with batteries and an electric motor, are also much more fuel-efficient than today's vehicles. They offer large potential fuel savings and low emissions. The Honda *Insight,* recently introduced in the U.S., gets more than sixty miles per gallon in cities and more than seventy on highways. Thus EVs and hybrids are a powerful weapon against smog, global warming, and acid rain.

Solar Thermal Electric Power Plants

Solar thermal electric power plants concentrate sunlight on a heat receiver and then convey the heat to an engine that converts it to mechanical power and electricity. There are three major types of solar thermal plants: the trough concentrator, the dish/engine concentrator, and the solar power tower. While the first of these is already commercial, dish/engine plants are on the verge of commercial use, and solar power towers are five to ten years from limited introduction.

Solar Troughs

A million mirrors lie shimmering in the Mojave Desert sunlight. Stretching toward the horizon, they are reminiscent of an enormous computer chip on the flat, California desert floor. These are the energy collection systems for nine solar thermal electric trough plants which have been in commercial operation since the 1980s.

These power plants with their trough-shaped collectors are solar-fossil "hybrids" that not only turn the Sun's heat into electricity, but also burn natural gas for cloudy-day or nighttime operation. With a combined electrical generating capacity of 354 MW, the plants send enough power over utility lines to meet the electrical needs of a small city. Three-quarters of the plants' yearly output is produced from sunlight; only a quarter from natural gas. The output peaks in the afternoon when customer demand in the Southern California Edison service area reaches a peak.

By adding a modest amount of low-cost heat storage, or by including biogas or hydrogen fuel backup capability for cloudy periods, solar thermal electric power plants can operate cleanly and continuously, in spite of short-term variations in sunlight.

This reliable utility-scale technology could produce huge amounts of electricity given the availability of vast areas of hot desert land throughout the southwestern U.S. and northwestern Mexico. Only a small fraction of the desert would be sufficient to produce more power than the U.S. now consumes. Current costs are 10-12 cents per kilowatt-hour, twice the cost of coal power, but major cost reductions are possible through mass production, further research, and construction of larger plants.[9]

Dish/Engines

Solar energy can be served from a dish as well as a trough. The solar dish concentrator uses a dish-shaped mirror or mirrors to heat a pressurized gas to more than 1,300°F. The contained gas expands and contracts to drive the piston of an engine that operates a generator or alternator to produce electricity.

Solar dish/engines are the most efficient of any solar electric power technology. They are also very reliable, relatively quiet, easily installed, and come in relatively small sizes that can be scaled up or used in groups. Solar dish/engine systems can be easily hybridized with natural gas or biogas for backup power production. Plants like this could be sited in suburban areas of the southwestern U.S. for utility "grid support."

The Tower of Power

Within a few years, another type of solar electric power plant, the "solar power tower", will enter the commercial arena. This plant uses a field of Sun-tracking mirrors that concentrate sunlight from many angles on a tower-mounted heat receptor. From there the energy goes to power an electric generator, or to a tank of molten salt that stores solar energy for cloudy day and nighttime operation.

Power towers have higher temperatures and higher efficiencies than trough plants. Currently, they are also the only solar thermal technology to offer significant thermal energy storage. In 1999, Solar Two, a 10-MW pilot plant operating at Barstow, California, for the first time successfully delivered grid-connected electricity around-the-clock using a molten salt energy storage system. The DOE expects the costs of electricity from power towers to fall to the four cents a kilowatt-hour range by 2030.

Electricity from Solar Cells

Photovoltaic devices, commonly called solar cells or PVs, turn light directly into electricity without fuel, fire, carbon dioxide, or pollution of any kind. They are also silent, use no water, have no moving parts to break down, and their main ingredient is recyclable silicon, the second most common element on Earth. Solar cell technology can thus contribute energy cleanly and indefinitely.

Another of PV's advantages is that, like most renewable technologies, it makes use of domestic resources and therefore produces domestic jobs and creates valuable economic impacts. It cannot be curtailed by foreign whim or embargo and offers opportunities for the profitable export of environmentally beneficial technologies.

Solar Cells in Action
Solar cells are not only simple to use and produce relatively few environmental impacts but are an extremely versatile technology. They provide commercial electricity for utility-scale power plants; they generate on-site power for homes, offices, and schools; and they serve off-grid remote power needs. They are cost-competitive for these

remote uses and for a myriad of specialty applications, such as providing power for satellites, highway call boxes, traffic signs, street lights, signal buoys, and offshore oil drilling platforms.

Solar electric panels can be installed on rooftops or as an integral part of a building's roof, walls, or window glass. Used in this manner—providing power while "clothing" the building—PV panels help defray costs of structural materials, such as roofing, windows, and wall cladding. PV panels also add design accents to a building's facade while thin-film modules integrated in window glazing can provide attractively diffuse day-lighting.

When grid-connected, modules can provide for all or part of a building's electrical needs; the power grid serves as a backup power source and as a conduit through which to sell unneeded power. Solar panels can also be used as emergency power supplies to guard against system-wide power outages.

Although ten million U.S. homes have sufficient sunshine and suitable unshaded roofs to produce 30,000 MW of solar electricity annually, only about 100,000 American homes are currently equipped with photovoltaic panels.

To create a PV power plant, large numbers of modules are interconnected into groups mounted on simple support structures, with or without tracking devices to keep each unit aimed at the Sun for maximum power production. Since modules are factory-built, solar plants can be constructed very rapidly, compared with fossil fuel plants. Once installed, solar power plants require minimal attention as the cells are long-lived and highly reliable.

The Environmental Payoff

Every four-kilowatt photovoltaic system installed on a residential rooftop in a sunny location avoids the emission of 282,000 pounds of carbon dioxide, 1,500 pounds of sulfur oxides, and 900 pounds of nitrogen oxides during its life, compared to the emissions produced when four kilowatts are generated by conventional means.[10]

Present and Future Solar Cell Costs

Despite the fact that PV is currently the most expensive of the commercial renewable energy technologies, costs have fallen steeply from $1,000 per peak watt in the 1960s to only $3 per peak watt in 1999. Advances in solar technology and manufacturing are likely to further reduce the production cost of PV to a tenth of today's levels.

Thus, with continued research and development support, by the time most of today's power plants are due for replacement, it should be possible to generate power from photovoltaic systems for as little as five cents a kilowatt-hour. Once the costs of solar electric systems are reduced to levels more competitive with coal, gas, and oil, PV growth should soar. It is therefore destined to become a very important global energy source within the next few decades.

Geothermal Energy

Geothermal energy is produced mainly from the ancient heat in the Earth's core remaining from the planet's formation billions of years ago and, to a lesser extent, from the radioactive decay of elements within the Earth. The friction of geologic plates sliding beneath each other at continental margins also supplies geothermal energy, as does the Sun, which warms the upper few feet of the Earth's crust.

Because geothermal power plants tap into the Earth's underground heat sources, they have no need to burn fuel and make no significant contribution to global warming or acid rain. They employ reliable, carbon-free technology that produces round-the-clock power on demand at very reasonable and declining costs.

Geothermal energy can provide industrial process heat, electricity, and direct heating and cooling for buildings. Some ninety-five percent of Iceland's buildings are geothermally warmed as are buildings in at least twenty U.S. cities that use geothermal district heating systems. Their customers typically save 30-50 percent on heating bills.

Geothermal energy is found as shallow reservoirs of below-ground hot water and steam, as deeper hot dry rock, as pressurized gas-laden brine, and as molten rock. The exploitation of hydrothermal (hot water) resources is already a mature technology. But these are virtually the only geothermal resources we are exploiting today, and we are tapping only a small portion of them.

Known U.S. hydrothermal deposits could produce about 23,000 MW of electrical capacity. Yet-to-be discovered U.S. hydrothermal reserves could generate 95,000-150,000 MW for 30 years, according to the U.S. Geological Survey. But this large resource is dwarfed by the enormity of the hot, dry rock geothermal resource. The engineering feasibility of extracting energy from it has been demonstrated, but further research and development is needed to make the technology commercially cost-competitive.

The hot, dry rock resource is believed to be large enough to supply current U.S. electrical demand for up to half a million years. Geothermal energy thus ultimately could prove to be among the nation's most valuable energy resources, offering us a colossal energy payback in the form of pollution-free energy wherever advanced drilling technology could reach the hot rock formations. Regrettably, when federal energy research and development money is handed out, geothermal energy receives far less than its potential justifies—about ten percent of an all-too-small energy R&D budget.

Energy Efficiency as a Resource

To the extent that efficiency improvements "liberate" unused energy and make it available to do other work, energy efficiency can be viewed as an energy resource. The efficiency gains possible in the U.S. and other economies are a huge resource that we can draw upon for years without exhausting it.

A 1991 study at Lawrence Berkeley National Laboratory found that up to forty percent of U.S. home energy demand could be elimi-

Table 3: Electricity and Fuel Possible from U.S. Renewable Energy Sources in 2030[11]

Energy Source	Energy Service	Quantity
Existing Renewables (Year 2000)	Electricity	ca. 100,000 MW
Biomass*	Electricity	100,000 MW
	Ethanol	More than sufficient to supply all cars and light trucks
	Methanol	More than sufficient to supply all cars and light trucks
Hydropower Upgrades	Electricity	20,000 MW
Geothermal		
Hydrothermal	Electricity	25,000 MW
Hot Dry Rock	Electricity	5,000 MW
Solar Thermal	Electricity	150,000 MW[†]
Photovoltaic	Electricity	100,000 MW[‡]
Wind	Electricity	200,000 MW[§]

Total Electrical Capacity   700,000 MW

Total Liquid Fuel Production   More than sufficient to supply all cars and light trucks

Total Carbon Emission Reduction in Electricity Sector: >90%[¥]
Total Net Carbon Emissions from Cars and Trucks: Near-zero

Note: Total electricity requirements in year 2000 are 829,000 MW.
1 MW = One million watts
See page 120 for notes to this table.

nated through investments in energy efficiency that were cheaper than the average cost of residential electricity. Even the industrial sector harbors many undeveloped efficiency opportunities.[12]

In the electricity sector, the efficiency of electric power generation can be doubled using available technology, thereby halving carbon emissions. This will take time, as equipment will have to be replaced, and power plants usually take 20-40 years to wear out.[13]

Desirable as energy efficiency is, merely increasing it is not enough to solve the carbon emission problem. As historical trends reveal, despite enormous increases in efficiency, world energy use has soared 450 percent just since 1950 and is projected to double again by 2030. By 2100 it is expected to grow 400 percent over 1995 levels if present trends continue. The trend is not our friend.

Moreover, whereas investment in energy efficiency is often effective in cutting carbon emissions in the short-term, efficiency investments do not fix the economy's continued dependence on carbon-based energy sources. As population and economic growth continue, energy use will burgeon, far outpacing growth in energy efficiency. Carbon emissions will thus continue rising. The purchase of energy efficiency thus buys time and mitigates damages, but it fails to eliminate the underlying problem.

From Each Region According to Its Ability

To build a cost-effective renewable energy system, each technology should be sited where the natural resources it requires are of the best quality and where markets are accessible. For example, to produce wind power economically in the U.S., wind farms should be sited in California, Texas, the Great Plains, and the Northeast, where winds are strongest and where existing facilities are able to deliver the added load to power markets.

Solar thermal power plants should be sited in the southwestern U.S. and in northern Mexican deserts where skies are clear and sunlight is intense. Photovoltaic panels initially should be sited on sunny southwestern and midwestern rooftops and integrated into upscale commercial buildings where PV costs can be a relatively minor part of total investment costs.

Biomass should be co-fired at existing coal-burning facilities. In the Northeast, Midwest, and Southeast—where agricultural and forest resources are plentiful—biomass should be gasified for use in combined-cycle plants, fuel cells, and for blending with natural gas. Biogas production should be expanded at landfills and other sites where large volumes of organic material decompose. Once advanced processes are commercialized for converting biomass to liquid alcohol fuels, alcohol-producing facilities should be sited near large sources of wood wastes and near future energy crop plantations.

Additional hydropower should be produced at existing dams through repowering, without increasing environmental harm.

Taken together, the measures described in this chapter would dramatically increase our renewable generating capacity, enabling the nation to reduce its energy imports, enhance its energy security, protect the climate, and prosper economically.

Time to Make Better Choices

Overloading the atmosphere with carbon is not an inexorable process. It is caused by conscious energy choices. Until now, those choices have been made according to narrow economic criteria—which fuels are most profitable for sellers and cheapest for buyers? But we need not project this shortsighted practice into the future. By developing a national consensus that these criteria must be revised and broadened, we can make better energy choices. For we now have potent tools with which to crack down on excess carbon emissions, and the economic resources to build a clean, modern energy system. Chapter 6 describes the steps we must take to do so.

CHAPTER SIX

Creating A Clean-Energy Future

By the time we're absolutely certain about the threat of rapid climate change, it will be too late to avert its dangers. So we must take effective precautionary action now.

That's where renewable energy technologies and efficiency come in. Public policies must be developed that will enable these emission-reducers to fulfill their exciting potential. A realistic strategy will also be needed for getting these policies adopted. So we'll look here at steps that governments must take, and at what you can do to help mobilize them. But first, what can we do in our own lives to help protect the climate?

Personal Actions

More than twenty-two tons of carbon dioxide and equivalent gases are released yearly for each citizen of the U.S.—more than in every nation in the world but Australia, Luxembourg, and the carbon-rich United Arab Emirates. Yet just by taking practical measures, each of us can reduce our emissions by as much as five and a half tons. Here are some suggestions:[1]

1. **Your biggest opportunity occurs when you buy a car.**
   Switching to a fuel-efficient car—rated at 32 miles per gallon or more—can reduce heat-trapping gas emissions by as much as 5,600 pounds per year. This will also save you money on gasoline, while reducing U.S. dependence on distant energy sources. Switching to one of the new hybrid-electric vehicles will have an even greater impact.

2. **Save energy at home.** Use a timer or adjust your thermostat when no one is going to be home to avoid heating or cooling an empty house. Close heating and air conditioning ducts to seldom-used rooms. Make sure windows are sealed and weather-stripped, and that exterior walls and roofs are insulated along with water heater and hot water pipes. Install energy efficient shower heads that use less hot water. These steps can eliminate more than 1.2 tons of carbon dioxide emissions per year and will greatly reduce utility bills.

3. **Improve lighting efficiency.** Use task lighting, such as desk lamps, when possible rather than overall room lighting. Substitute lower-wattage bulbs. Install dimmer switches so you can adjust illumination. When selecting light fixtures, remember that fluorescents put out the same amount of light as incandescents at a third the energy, and since they last ten times as long, you'll save money as well as energy. For new buildings, consider skylights, light shelves, and light pipes—all of which bring natural light inside and enhance comfort.

4. **Recycle.** Recycling household newsprint, cardboard, glass, and metal can reduce your emissions of carbon dioxide by 850 pounds each year. According to the Sierra Club, each four-foot-high stack of newspapers that you recycle saves one tree.

5. **Use recycled products.** Their production consumes 70-90 percent less energy than comparable new materials. For example, producing recycled paper requires only one-fifth the energy used to make paper from newly cut trees. Also, purchase products packaged in containers using recycled materials.

6. **Purchase clean household power.** If you can select your energy supplier thanks to restructuring of the utility industry, chose one that provides "green," renewably-generated power.

7. **Use renewable energy.** Consider solar-powered home

lighting when you install or upgrade exterior lighting. If you are building a new home, have it designed to take advantage of opportunities for solar water and space heating and photovoltaic panels. A solar water heater can reduce household carbon dioxide emissions by over 700 pounds a year.

8. **Plant trees.** According to the Sierra Club, planting just three shade trees around your house can cut your air conditioning energy use by as much as half. If the trees are deciduous rather than evergreen, they will not only cool your house in the summer, but will also allow the Sun to warm your house in the winter, after their leaves have fallen. If you cannot plant trees yourself, you may want to contact one of several organizations with tree-planting programs, such as American Forests' Global ReLeaf (www.americanforests.org).

9. **Use public transit.** Carbon dioxide releases can amount to about 9,000 pounds every 15,000 miles for most passenger cars. Large sport utility vehicles, release more than twice that much—about 1.3 pounds every mile.

10. **Use energy-efficient appliances.** Many appliances now carry a yellow and black efficiency rating label. Refrigerators and washing machines in particular have large energy requirements. Replacing them with high-efficiency models can reduce carbon dioxide emissions by nearly 700 pounds a year.

11. **Switch to human power.** Many of the tasks for which we have come to depend on power equipment can be done just as well or better with manual tools. Just putting away your power mower and using a push mower instead will save eighty pounds a year in carbon dioxide emissions.

12. **Eat responsibly grown, local produce.** Avoiding food shipped long distances will reduce the large amounts of energy consumed in transportation. So will choosing organic foods that are produced without energy-intensive pesticides, herbicides, and synthetic fertilizers.

13. **Reduce consumption of meat.** Producing animal calories requires a great deal more land, water, soil, and energy than plant calories and results in large releases of heat-trapping methane to the atmosphere. By replacing meat in your diet in favor of grains, fruits, and vegetables, you will decrease the energy needed in food production while reducing your risk of heart attack, stroke, and cancer.

14. **Avoid CFCs.** Chlorofluorocarbons (CFCs) are very powerful greenhouse gases that also destroy ozone. Current laws require them to be phased out, but some products still contain them. If your auto air conditioner or refrigerator contains CFCs and needs service, make sure the company you hire recycles the refrigerant. Don't buy fire extinguishers containing halons, another powerful greenhouse gas.

15. **Vote with your pocketbook.** Consider a company's position on climate change issues when you decide where to spend your money. Reward good corporate citizens with your patronage and, if you decide not to patronize a firm, let the management know your reasoning.

16. **Join up.** Become an active member of a citizen action organization or environmental group. Appendix A: Gathering Support to Prevent a Climate Crisis, will point you toward an organization in your area. For more comprehensive information, see the author's list of organizations and resources at the *Beating the Heat* website: www.berkeleyhills.com/beatingtheheat.

17. **Get politically involved.** Learn about climate-related issues that impact your community and inform your political representatives and candidates about them. Attend meetings of public bodies, such as city councils, school boards, boards of supervisors and influence them to take appropriate action. Appendix A will give you basic tools needed to do this effectively.

Setting Policies: Ground Rules for a Clean-Energy Revolution

For renewable energy use to spread through our economy and cut carbon emissions permanently, clean energy must be made cheaper to the buyer and more profitable to the seller than fossil fuels. Once this is accomplished, we can stand back as powerful market forces take over and expand the nation's renewable energy supplies.

To make this possible, we need to set ground rules that encourage competition and innovation, while ensuring that markets serve the public, rather than the other way around. The rules needed are comparable to those that apply to the deregulated airline, natural gas, telecommunications, and trucking industries.

Deregulation, which is currently revolutionizing electric utilities, does not literally mean "no regulations." It means keeping them to a minimum, consistent with protection of public health and safety, and with fair competition. The rules for deregulated energy markets should incorporate certain core principles:

- The polluter must pay for both the environmental and economic damages caused by his pollution.
- Subsidies to mature polluting technologies—be they fossil or nuclear—should be phased out.
- Precaution must prevail when rules are written affecting the environment, and public health and safety. Emission limits must be set low enough, and emission charges must be set high enough, to guarantee that the climate is protected.

Defining an Energy Strategy

To achieve a safe energy economy as quickly as possible, we need to use an energy strategy that has a little pull, a little push, and a little pinch in it. Such a strategy would pull renewables into the marketplace and push fossil fuels out. It would also pinch off energy demand, but without curtailing energy services or life-styles.

Market pull policies would include major investments in renewable energy research and development, a minimum renewable energy requirement for utilities, tax credits for renewable energy producers, investment tax credits, accelerated depreciation for certain energy-related investments, long-term renewable power purchases by governments, and public education programs.

The push part of the strategy has two segments designed to constrain fossil fuel use. First, an outright prohibition on construction of new coal-burning facilities until emissions of carbon dioxide can be eliminated (or vastly reduced) through carbon capture and storage.

Second, shrinking carbon emission caps for power plants and other energy using facilities. These tradable permits would make fossil fuel energy more expensive and would thus reduce demand, pushing fossil fuel power out of the market. As older plants are retired, and the national ceiling on emissions gets progressively lower, replacements would then be primarily renewable.

A simpler method than carbon caps for speeding the departure of the old technologies would be a direct per ton carbon emission fee, a policy that various European nations have adopted.[2]

The "pinching" part of the strategy comprises a family of policies designed to enhance the economy's energy efficiency, so as to constrain energy waste and pinch off unnecessary demand.

To be successful, a renewable energy strategy will need to minimize the amount of public financial support needed. Public resources should thus be focused on reducing the cost gap between renewables and their competitors. As the relative price of renewables falls, market demand for them will rise. Private capital will then come forward to create more renewable generating capacity. Public funds will go much farther this way than if used to buy entire renewable generating systems outright.

Policies for Protecting The Climate

1. **Phase out all public subsidies to the fossil fuel and nuclear industries.** This will free tens of billions of dollars of taxpayers' money annually. Redirect the savings to fund nonpolluting energy sources. In 1989, federal energy subsidies ranged from $21 to $36 billion a year, with almost ninety percent going to mature, conventional energy sources rather than to emerging solar and wind technologies. This figure does not include an estimated $50 billion a year in military expenses for the defense of U.S. international oil interests.

2. **Give producers of electricity from nonpolluting energy sources generous energy production tax credits or incentive payments.** A production tax credit was created by the National Energy Policy Act of 1992 (EPAct), but it provides only 1.7 cents a kilowatt-hour to commercial wind and biomass energy producers for the first ten years of plant operation, and no incentives for solar or geothermal power.

3. **Provide expanded tax credits that stimulate investment in certified renewable energy technologies.** EPAct now provides only a ten percent investment tax credit for equipment that uses solar energy to generate electricity or for heating and cooling. The credit could easily be raised to twenty-five percent or more. (For ten years, Denmark allowed a thirty percent investment tax credit for the purchase of wind turbines. The credit is no longer necessary and has been phased out; the Danish wind industry now dominates world wind turbine markets.)

4. **Give consumers tax credits for choosing green power.** Rewarding consumers for choosing environmentally desirable energy sources—rather than penalizing them by higher prices, as occurs today—will spur the market for green power.

5. **Establish a national wires charge for each kilowatt-hour of

nonrenewably generated electricity. A one cent per kilowatt-hour charge nationwide would yield $30 billion for investment in renewable energy. This would also help compensate for the forty-five percent drop in energy efficiency investment by utilities that followed the onset of deregulation in 1993.[3]

6. **Establish a national minimum renewable energy requirement.** Anyone who sells electricity in the U.S. would have to provide a steadily increasing proportion of their power from nonpolluting sources, or purchase surplus renewable energy credits earned by others. Starting with only a small percentage of the total power offered, the standard would gradually rise until all major new additions to generating capacity would be from renewable sources. Currently ten states have a minimum renewable energy requirement.

7. **Phase out fossil fuel plants that cannot meet new emission standards.** This step would quickly wring excess electric generating capacity out of the system and would increase demand for new generation that renewables could fill.

8. **Ban construction of new coal-fired plants.** As a short-term expedient, allow the conversion of existing coal-fired plants to natural gas, wherever practicable. Substitution of natural gas for coal in power plants should reduce carbon emissions from these sources by roughly half.

9. **Implement a tax on carbon emissions as Denmark, Finland, Netherlands, Norway, and Sweden have done.** The carbon tax could be made more politically palatable if its proceeds were used to directly reduce payroll taxes. It would thus be revenue-neutral, but would shift taxes from labor to pollution.

10. **Establish a National Renewable Energy Bank to make low-interest loans for renewable energy projects.** Often the cost and availability of money is critical to a renewable energy project, especially for technologies such as solar electric and

wind, where the majority of the costs are up-front investments, while fuel, operation, and maintenance costs are low.

11. **Expand renewable energy and energy efficiency research and development.** In fiscal year 2000, Congress appropriated only $321 million for renewable energy (less than $1.20 per person) for a nation with an $8.5 trillion Gross National Product.

12. **Shift federal government energy purchases from nonrenewable to renewable sources.** The federal government purchases $8 billion worth of energy per year. Shouldn't the institution that sets national environmental standards buy its energy from the most environmentally responsible sources?

13. **Hold stranded investments hostage to stranded benefits.** As the utility industry is deregulated nationwide, utilities are demanding to be repaid for earlier "stranded investments" in coal and nuclear plants that are no longer competitive. At the same time, utilities are abandoning prior commitments to support energy efficiency and renewable energy research and development—"stranded benefits." The recovery of "stranded" costs should not be permitted until these benefits are revitalized and guaranteed for the long-term.

14. **Establish national net metering regulations.** Such regulations make it easy for households and other small generators of renewable energy to receive credits for selling back renewable power they generate to their energy provider, paying only for the net power consumed. Currently, thirty states have net metering laws, and several proposals for federal net metering legislation are being considered in Congress.

15. **Establish fair transmission rules for renewable energy.** Current rules can be prejudicial to intermittent renewables, forcing them to pay transmission charges whether they use distribution facilities at a particular time or not.

16. **Disclose energy sources and their emissions to utility**

customers with their utility bills, so they can make informed decisions about their energy supplies. Many customers who would support clean technologies are not aware of the environmental impacts of their energy sources.

17. **Require that "green power" providers be properly certified.** This will help prevent the sale of nonrenewable energy under a phony green banner. Currently the nonprofit Center for Resource Solutions (www.resource-solutions.org) has an accreditation program for utility green power plans.

18. **Modernize and upgrade turbines and generators of existing hydroelectric facilities.** This should make another 20,000 MW of renewable electrical power available to the economy at minimal environmental cost.[4]

19. **Reduce emissions of methane and nitrous oxide from agriculture.** Agriculture now produces about fifty percent of the world's human-generated methane releases and seventy percent of its human-generated nitrous oxide emissions.[5] We need to seriously consider establishing methane and nitrous oxide permit systems for industry and agriculture analogous to the hugely successful sulfur dioxide permits currently used in the electricity generating sector. Over the past twenty years, they have slashed sulfur dioxide emissions in half.

20. **Use international trading mechanisms to reduce carbon emissions.** Inasmuch as investments in emissions control are often much cheaper in developing nations, international emissions trading opportunities should be fully utilized to take advantage of as much emission avoidance as possible.

21. **Speed the transfer of energy efficiency and renewable energy technologies to developing nations.** Just as we ought not export pesticides and pharmaceuticals banned for use in the United States, neither should we export polluting fossil fuel technologies under the guise of helping other nations.

22. **Halt massive, worldwide forest clearance and degradation.**

The U.S. needs to support aggressive global efforts to halt tropical deforestation. We also must enhance global and domestic efforts to restore forest cover by reforestation and by assisting natural forest regeneration.[6]

Some of the policies described here already exist. Many states offer renewable energy incentives, and a few utilities also provide financial incentives, including grants, rebates, and equipment leases to encourage customer use of renewable energy. But our current patchwork of pro-renewable energy policies needs to be far better coordinated and vastly strengthened.

Taking Responsibility for Change

Obviously it will not be enough to simply identify an ensemble of "correct policies," and then sit back and wait for them to be mysteriously adopted. Six billion people now live on Earth, and most of us, to varying degrees, are contributing to the disruption of the global carbon cycle. A popular mass movement is necessary if we are to protect the climate and restore damaged resources.

Each of us can take some responsibility for reducing lethal impacts on the Earth and for recruiting others to follow this path. If every reader of this book makes a commitment to help address this problem, and shares their concerns with others, we will have an impact on climate policy and, hopefully, will avert a catastrophe.

Can ordinary citizens *really* make a difference? It is amazing that in a world of some six billion people, a single, deeply committed individual, acting out of concern for the Earth and the common good, still has great influence. The national parks, wilderness areas, Wild and Scenic Rivers, and World Heritage Sites attest to the phenomenal power of concerned citizens who guided or prevailed upon large national governments and other huge institutions.

These protected areas and our environmental laws were not

dreamed up by corporations who felt they were polluting too much or wanted to place natural resources beyond their own reach. Resources were protected and environmental statutes were passed through the work of individuals who labored with a burning passion and unswerving dedication. You, too, have the power to have an impact.

Where to Start?

Could you bring your life into harmony with your vision of a climate-safe, clean-energy world? Daily or frequent small steps as outlined earlier in this chapter can carry us a long way toward the goal.

Next comes public involvement in the struggle for a sustainable world. Many groups already working to protect the climate and promote safe energy will enthusiastically welcome your participation. (See Appendix A.) Or, once you have become as knowledgeable as you can about the issues, you may find that no one is effectively addressing those about which you feel most strongly. It might be necessary to start a new campaign or even a new organization.

You need not become an expert or a professional to do so. Basic facts and perseverance will do. Perhaps your campaign could aim to reduce the emissions of a local corporation, to influence the energy practices of local government, to improve public transit, to establish national minimum renewable energy requirements, or even to advance international efforts to set a cap on heat-trapping gas emissions. Whether or not you attain your entire goal, you will learn a great deal, make progress, and inspire others.

A Call to Activism

To understand how popular activism can bring about change, consider a recent successful challenge to one of the world's largest retailers. Citizens led by the Sierra Club and Greenpeace persuaded

Home Depot to agree to phase out its sales of old growth lumber. The activists were creative and committed. They bombarded Home Depot with 25,000 postcards, brought their "Great Bear Rain Forest" exhibit bus to the company's stockholders' meeting, and put up a Home Depot bulletin board on a forest clear-cut near Vancouver.[7]

In the same way, you and groups you belong to can use your collective power to influence companies that deny global warming, flagrantly pollute the atmosphere, or oppose climate safety measures. Boycotts educate the public and media while they pressure companies and politicians to take actions that the climate crisis requires.

Activists also can organize "teach-ins" on clean energy and climate safety on college campuses and in town hall meetings to acquaint people with the issues and the solutions. When broadcast on the Internet, the meetings could be used not only to inform and respond to the community, but also to develop realistic local and national strategies for change.

Cause for Hope

The carbon fuels at the source of our human-induced carbon emissions are produced by a surprisingly small number of enormously wealthy companies. Only 122 of these energy titans supply eighty percent of the entire world's carbon from coal, oil, and natural gas.[8] Twenty of these companies produce fifty percent of the world's total carbon. This is both good news and bad.

These giant carbon merchants will not hasten to abandon profitable businesses. They live off fossil fuel revenues. Neither coddling nor appeasement will sway them. In fact, halfhearted policies actually work to their advantage by creating the illusion that the underlying problems are being fixed. But bold policies with broad-based political support will eventually have their intended effect. When the powerful are few, they are vulnerable.

Parting Words

In *Beating the Heat*, we have seen the havoc that rapid climate change could bring. We have identified the culprit: rampant fossil fuel use. We have learned that the solution lies in creating a clean energy economy. To do so, we need a bold energy policy that provides market incentives for renewable technologies and energy efficiency, and strong financing for clean energy research. Designing these policies is a straightforward exercise.

The difficult questions we face are political. Are we resolute enough to demand clean-energy policies and insist on their adoption? Are we willing to take on entrenched fossil fuel industries and their allies? If not, the atmosphere's carbon dioxide burden is likely to reach three times pre-industrial levels by the end of this century.

Decisive action is required. Under a business-as-usual forecast, renewable energy's share of total worldwide energy use will not increase much, if at all, for at least the next two decades.[1]

Clearly we cannot afford to sit still for another twenty years. Those of us who are concerned about climate change must convince our leadership and fellow citizens to oppose the powerful interests who are perpetuating the carbon economy. We must alter the fossil fuel-oriented energy policies that reflect the undue influence of corporations and the failure of government to resist it.

The proposals in chapter six and the strategies and tactics in the back of this book tell how to start the energy transformation. They can set in motion a massive and irresistible constituency for climate-safe, clean energy. Everyone can be a part of this effort. Everyone truly has a stake in its success.

Endnotes

Chapter Three: Counting the Costs

1. Fankhauser, S., 1995. *Valuing climate change. The economics of the greenhouse*, Earthscan, London
   Tol, R.S.J., 1995. The damage costs of climate change: Towards more comprehensive calculations, *Environmental and Resource Economics*, 5, 353-374; and others.
   Cline, W.R., 1992. *The economics of global warming*, Institute for International Economics, Washington, DC.
2. Rind, D., D. Goldberg, J. Hansen, C. Rosenzweig, and R. Ruedy, 1990. Potential evapotranspiration and the likelihood of future drought. *Journal of Geophysical Research* 95(D7), 9,983-10,004.
   Kane, S., J. Reilly, and J. Tobey, 1992. An empirical study of the economic effects of climate change on world agriculture, *Climatic Change* 21, 17-35.
   Rosenzweig, C., M. Parry, K. Frohberg, and G. Fisher, 1993. *Climate change and world food supply,* Environmental Change Unit, Oxford.
3. Cline, W.R., 1992. *The economics of global warming*, Institute for International Economics, Washington, DC.
4. *Climate Change 1995 — Economic and Social Dimensions of Climate Change.* Contribution of Working Group III to the Second Assessment Report of the Intergovernmental Panel on Climate Change. J.P. Bruce, H. Lee, and E.F.Haites (eds.). Cambridge, England: Cambridge University Press.
   Myers, N., 1993. Environmental refugees in a globally warmer world. *BioScience,* 43 (11),752-761.
5. Gleick, P.H., 1992. *Water and conflict.* Project on Environmental Change and Acute Conflict, University of Toronto and the American Academy of Arts and Science. Cambridge, MA.
   Homer-Dixon, T.F., J.H. Boutwell, and G.W. Rathjens, 1993. Environmental change and violent conflict, *Scientific American*, 268(2), 38-45.
6. Gleick, P.H., 1987. Regional hydrologic consequences of increases in atmospheric CO_2 and other trace gases, *Climate Change* 10; 137-161.
   Gleick, P. H. and L.L. Nash, 1991. *The societal and environmental costs of the continuing California drought.* Pacific Institute for Studies in Development, Environment and Security. Oakland, CA.
7. Cline 1992, *op. cit.*

Titus, J.G., 1992. The cost of climate change to the United States. In *Global climate change: Implications, challenges and mitigation measures*, S.K. Majumdar, L.S. Kalkstein, B. Yarnal, E.W. Miller, and L.M. Rosenfeld, (Eds.). Pennsylvania Academy of Science, Easton, PA.

8. Price, C., and D. Rind, 1994. The impact of a 2xCO$_2$ climate on lightning-caused fires, *Journal of Climate* 7, 1484-1494.

9. S. Fankhauser, 1995, *op. cit.*and other references cited in *Climate Change 1995*, Working Group III, *op. cit.*, Chapter 6.)

10. A twenty-inch rise is considered more probable by 2100 AD in response to a carbon dioxide doubling, with 40 inches regarded as a possible upper bound. But once the atmosphere is sufficiently altered, seas will continue rising long after 2100 AD. Sooner or later, they will have risen by 40 inches, and the economic consequences will have to be faced.

11. *Climate Change 1995 — Economic and Social Dimensions of Climate Change, op. cit.*, Chapter 6, p. 199.

12. U.S. Environmental Protection Agency, 1989. *The potential effects of global climate change in the United States*. J.B. Smith and D. Tirpak, eds. Washington, DC.
    Cline 1992, *op. cit.*
    Titus 1992, *op. cit.*

13. Dobson, A., A. Jolly, and D. Rubenstein, 1989. The greenhouse effect and biological diversity. *Trends in Ecology and Evolution*, 4(3) 64-68.

14. Lettenmaier, D.P. and N. Mantua, 1998. "Potential Consequences of Global Warming for the Northwestern U.S.: Water Resources and Marine Ecosystems." U.S. Global Change Research Program Seminar. May 13.

15. *Climate Change 1995 — Economic and Social Dimensions of Climate Change, op. cit.*, Chapter 6.

16. Alley, R.B. and P.B.deMenocal, 1998. "Abrupt Climate Changes Revisted: How Serious and How Likely?" U.C. Global Change Research Program Seminar. February 17.

17. Berger, J.J., 1990. *Evaluating Ecological Protection and Restoration Projects: A Holistic Approach to the Assessment of Complex, Multi-Attribute Resource Management Problems.* Ph.D. Dissertation. University of California, Davis.

18. Working Group on Public Health and Fossil-Fuel Combustion, 1997. "Short-term improvements in public health from global-climate policies on fossil-fuel combustion: an interim report," *Lancet*, Nov. 8, pp. 1341-1348.
    World Resources Institute, 1997. "The Hidden Benefits of Climate Policy: Reducing Fossil Fuel Use Saves Lives Now." *Environmental Health Notes.* December.

Chapter Four: Myths and Mythmakers

1. Gelbspan, R., 1997. *The Heat is On.* Addison-Wesley: Reading, MA.
    Environmental Media Services and Environmental Media Center. *The
    1996 Media Guide to Climate Change* (at www.ems.org).
2. Park, R. L., 1998. "Scientists and Their Political Passions." *New York
    Times.* May 2.
    Associated Press, 1998. "Names Added to Greenhouse Plea."
    Firor, J. W., 1998. "Using Phony Science to Discredit Global Warming."
    EDF Letter. Vol XXIX, No. 4. September.
3. Seitz, F., 1997. "Science Has Spoken: Global Warming is a Myth."
    December 4.
    Woodwell, G.M. and J. P. Holdren, J.P., 1998. "Climate Change Skeptics
    Are Wrong." *International Herald Tribune.* November 14-15.
    Rachel's Environment & Health Weekly #596. 1998. "A New
    Disinformation Campaign." April 30.
4. Burton, B and S. Rampton, 1998. "Thinking Globally, Acting Vocally:
    The International Conspiracy to Overheat the Earth." Center for Media
    & Democracy, Madison, WI, with research provided by the Clearing-
    house on Environmental Advocacy and Research, Washington, D.C.
5. Gelbspan, *op. cit.,* and Burton, B. and S. Rampton, 1998. *op. cit.*
6. Burton, B. and S. Rampton, 1998. *op. cit.*
7. Burton, B. and S. Rampton, 1998. *op. cit.*
8. Profiles based on research by the Clearinghouse on Environmental
    Advocacy and Reasearch (CLEAR), a project of the Environmental
    Working Group in Washington D.C.
    Hammond, K. 1997. "Wingnuts in Sheeps Clothing," Mojo Wire
    (www.bsd.mojones.com/news). December 4.
    Burton, B. and S. Rampton, 1998. *op.cit.*
    Gelbspan, R.,1997. *op.cit.*
9. *1996 Media Guide to Climate Change. A Summary of the Scientific
    Consensus on Climate Change.* Environmental Media Services
    (www.ems.org).
10. *Climate Change 1995 — Economic and Social Dimensions of Climate
    Change.* Contribution of Working Group III to the Second Assessment
    Report of the Intergovernmental Panel on Climate Change. J.P. Bruce, H.
    Lee, and E.F.Haites (eds.). Cambridge, England: Cambridge University
    Press.
    See also Intergovernmental Panel on Climate Change. 1998. *The
    Regional Impacts of Climate Change: An Assessment of Vulnerability.*
    Cambridge, England: Cambridge University Press.

11. Schneider, S.H., 1998. "Twisted Revision." *Washington Post*. January 7. p. A19.

12. Holdren, J. P. 1997. Excerpts from June 18 press conference in Washington, D.C., June 18. Published in *Global Change* by Pacific Institute for Studies in Development, Environment, and Security (Oakland, California).

13. Thomson, D.J., 1995. "The Seasons, Global Temperature, and Precession." *Science*, vol. 268, pp. 59-67.

14. Jones, P. D., 1990. "Assessment of Urbanization Effect in Time Series of Surface Air temperature over Land." *Nature*. Vol. 347, p. 169.
    Parker, D. E., *et al.* 1995. "Marine Surface Temperature: Observed Variations and Data Requirements." *Climate Change*. Vol. 31, p. 559.
    Jones, P. D., 1995. "Land Surface Temperatures—Is the Network Good Enough." *Climate Change.*, Vol. 31 p. 545.
    Climate Change 1995 — The Science of Climate Change. 1996. Intergovernmental Panel on Climate Change. Cambridge, MA, Cambridge University Press. pp. 142-143.

15. *Climate Change 1995 — The Science of Climate Change. op.cit.,* pp. 147-148.
    Wents, F. J. and Schabel, M., 1998. "Effects of Orbital Decay on Satellite Derived Lower Tropospheric Temperature Trends. " *Nature*. Vol. 394, p. 661.
    Spencer, R., 1998. "Measuring the Temperature of Earth from Space."Scientist's Notebook." *NASA Space Science News*. August 14.

16. *Climate Change 1995 — The Science of Climate Change. op.cit.,* p. 177.

17. For more on the theme that global warming is good for you, see Hoover Institution scholar Thomas Gale Moore's book: *Climate of Fear: Why We Shouldn't Worry About Global Warming.* Cato Institute, 1998.

18. Interlaboratory Working Group on Energy-Efficient and Low-Carbon Technologies. (Oak Ridge National Laboratory, Lawrence Berkeley National Laboratory, Pacific Northwest National Laboratory, National Renewable Energy Laboratory, and Argonne National Laboratory). 1997. *Scenarios of U.S. Carbon Reductions: Potential Impacts of Energy Technologies by 2010 and Beyond.* Prepared for Office of Energy Efficiency and Renewable Energy. U.S. Department of Energy. Interagency Analytical Team. 1997. *Economic Effects of Global Climate Change Policies.* Draft. May 30.
    Alliance to Save Energy, American Council for an Energy Efficient Economy, Natural Resources Defense Council, Tellus Institute, Union of Concerned Scientists. 1997. *Energy Innovations: A Prosperous Path to a Clean Environment.* June.

19. WEFA. 1998. *Global Warming: The High Cost of the Kyoto Protocal,*

National and State Impacts (Executive Summary). Prepared for the American Petroleum Institute. Eddystone, PA: WEFA, Inc.

20. Austin, D., J. Goldemberg, and G. Parker, 1998. "Contributions to Climate Change: Are Conventional Metrics Misleading the Debate?" *Climate Notes*. World Resources Institute. October.

21. Marland, G., T.A. Boden, R.J. Andres, A.L. Brenkert, and C.A. Johnston, 1999. Global, Regional, and National Fossil Fuel CO2 Emissions. In *Trends: A Compendium of Data on Global Change.* Carbon Dioxide Information Analysis Center, Oak Ridge National Laboratory. Oak Ridge, TN.

Chapter 5: Climate-Safe Energy Sources

1. Berger, J. J., 1997. *Charging Ahead: The Business of Renewable Energy and What it Means for America.* Berkeley, CA: University of California Press.

2. Berger, J. J., 1976. *Nuclear Power: The Unviable Option, A Critical Look At Our Energy Alternatives.* Palo Alto, CA: Ramparts Press; New York, NY: Dell Books, 1976.

3. International Energy Association, 1999. *The Evolving Renewable Energy Market.* The Netherlands: The Netherlands' Ministry of Economic Affairs, and the Netherlands Agency for Energy and the Environment). p. 11.

4. President's Committee of Advisors on Science and Technology. Panel on International Cooperation in Energy Research, Development, Demonstration, and Deployment, 1999. *Powerful Partnerships: The Federal Role in International Cooperation on Energy Innovation.* June.

5. Forty percent annually from 1993-1999, according to the American Wind Energy Asociation.

6. Department of Energy. Energy Efficency and Renewable Energy Network, 1999. "Solar Buildings Program." URL: www.eren.doe.gov/ solarbuildings/hotwater.html..

7. Solar Energy Research Institute, 1981. *A New Prosperity: Building a Sustainable Energy Future.* Andover, MA: Brick House Publishing. p. 2.

8. *Climate Change 1995 — Impacts, Adaptations and Mitigation of Climate Change, Scientific-Technical Analyses.* 1996. Intergovernmental Panel on Climate Change. Contribution of Working Group II. Energy Supply Mitigation Options. Cambridge, England: Cambridge University Press. Chapter 19, p. 607.

9. Berger, J. J. 1997. *op.cit.* and Office of Utility Technologies, Energy Efficiency and Renewable Energy and Electric Power Research Institute, December 1997. *Renewable Energy Technology Characterizations.* TR-109496.

10. See Sacramento Municipal Utility District. "PV Pioneer II Program FAQs." www.smud.org/home/pv_pioneer/FAQs.html. October 15, 1999.

11. Notes to Table 3.

    This table shows estimates of potential contributions of renewable energy to future U.S. energy supply assuming that energy efficiency technologies enable total energy demand to remain constant as population and energy services continue growing. We have also assumed that the remaining fossil-fueled electric generating plants rely on natural gas instead of coal or oil (or on gasified coal with carbon recapture) and that the natural gas plants' emissions are halved through the use of advanced combined-cycle turbine-generators.

    The numbers can be viewed as estimates of achievable but not necessarily one hundred percent commercially competitive electric supplies, unless policy measures are instituted that alter the apparent short-term cost advantage of fossil fuel technologies.

    The assumed addition of 20,000 MW per year of renewable energy generating capacity for thirty years (as was done for this table) is less than the average annual conventional generating capacity added to U.S. utility systems in the 1970s. Between 1970 and 1975, an average of 33,000 MW of new capacity was added to the U.S. utility system per year.

    Total final electricity requirements for year-2000 are assumed to be 829,000 MW (as in 1998) and, therefore, since 700,000 MW are renewably derived, the remaining 129,000 MW are assumed to be produced from fossil fuels, primarily combined-cycle gas turbines.

    *50 million acres of land in the U.S., much of it now idle, could be used to grow biomass sufficient to produce 100,000 MW of electrical power per year—twelve percent of U.S. 1998 generating capacity.

    † This projection is intermediate between PV and wind projections, reflecting the intermediate position of solar thermal electric costs relative to PV and wind.

    ‡ This assumes the current installed base of 8 MW grows at 37 percent per year, 2.5 times the current annual growth rate of U.S. solar cell shipments.

    § This assumes installed capacity increases to 100,000 MW in 2020 (comparable to growth projections made for Europe and 20 percent above Energy Information Administration 2020 projections for the U.S.) and that from 2020-2030, growth equals 7 percent, which is less than a quarter of the current global growth rate of wind power capacity.

    ¥ 129,000 MW of year-2030 capacity are produced by natural gas.

12. Koomey, J., et al. *The Potential for Electricity Efficiency Improvements in the United States Residential Sector.* Lawrence Berkeley Laboratory Report No. LBL-30477, Berkeley, CA. p.48. As cited *in Climate Change*

1995 — *Impacts, Adaptations and Mitigation of Climate Change, Scientific-Technical Analyses.* 1996. *op.cit.* Chapter 22, p. 741. Interlaboratory Working Group on Energy-efficient and Low-Carbon Technologies, 1997. *Scenarios of U.S. Carbon Reductions: Potential Impacts of Energy Technologies by 2010 and Beyond.* Washington DC, U.S Department of Energy.

13. *Climate Change 1995 — Impacts, Adaptations and Mitigation of Climate Change, Scientific-Technical Analyses.* 1996. *op.cit.*

Chapter Six: Creating a Clean-Energy Future

1. The suggestions in this table were distilled from information provided by the City of Portland Energy Office and the U.S. EPA, and the following sources:
    "21 Ways to Help Stop Global Warming," (a Sierra Club pamphlet).
    Leggett, J., 1990. *Global Warming: The Greenpeace Report.* Oxford/ New York, Oxford University Press.
    The Do It Yourself Guide to Combating Global Warming. The University of East Anglia Climate Research Unit's Tiempo Climate Cyberlibrary (www.cru.uea.ac.uk/tiempo/floor2/educ/diy /diy.htm).
    The Context Institute Website (www.context.org).

2. Brown, M.A., M.D. Levine, J.P. Romm, A.H. Rosenfeld, and J.G. Koomey, 1998. Engineering-Economic Studies of Energy Technologies to Reduce Greenhouse Gas Emissions: Opportunities and Challenges. *Annual Review of Energy and Environment.* Vol. 23, pp. 287-385.

3. Coequyt, J.R., R. Wiles, et al., 1998. *Unplugged: How Power Companies Have Abandoned Energy Efficiency Programs.* Washington DC, Environmental Working Group and World Wildlife Fund. October.

4. Interlaboratory Working Group. Office of Energy Efficiency and Renewable Energy. U.S. DOE. 1997. *Scenarios of U.S Carbon Reductions: Potential Impacts of Energy-Efficient and Low-Carbon Technologies by 2010 and Beyond.* Berkeley, CA, Lawrence Berkeley National Laboratory and Oak Ridge, TN, Oak Ridge National Laboratory. LBNL-40533 and ORNL-444. September.

5. Watson, R.T. , M.C. Zinyowera, and R.H. Moss, 1996. *Technical Paper I: Technologies, Policies and Measures for Mitigating Climate Change. Technical Summary.* Intergovernmental Panel on Climate Change, Working Group II.

6. See "Restoration Forestry," "Tropical Forests and International Forest Issues," and "Saving Forests" in Berger, J.J., 1998. *Understanding Forests.* San Francisco, CA: Sierra Club Books.

7. Brooke, J., 1999. Loggers Find Canada Rain Forest Flush With Foes. *New York Times*. October 22.

8. Natural Resources Defense Council, 1998. *The Kingpins of Carbon*. New York, NY.

Parting Words

1. This has been well documented by the International Energy Agency, the European Union, and the U.S. Department of Energy. See European Commission, December 1997. *Energy for the Future: Renewable Sources of Energy, White Paper for a Community Strategy and Action Plan,* and Energy Information Administration, U.S. Department of Energy, 1999. *International Energy Outlook 1999.*

Appendix A: Gathering Support to Prevent a Climate Crisis

If you'd like to express your views about climate change to energy decision makers in ways likely to bring about a swifter transition to a climate-safe, clean energy world, this chapter is for you. It tells how to get in touch with elected officials and how to influence local businesses, school districts, transit systems, and other regional and community institutions. At the end of the chapter, you'll also find a state-by-state list of the organizations that are most knowledgeable and active on energy and climate issues in each state. So wherever you live in the U.S., if you want to help protect the climate and safeguard the environment, all you need do to get started is to contact one of these groups.

The "Joys" of Lobbying

It has never been easier—nor more challenging—to lobby on energy and climate issues. Tools to help a citizen get oriented and stay informed are abundant; many environmental and advocacy organizations issue "activist alerts" and maintain web sites and telephone information "hotlines" with information on significant legislation. But the issues are more numerous and complex than ever. That's why it's good to work with existing organizations, even though some of these groups may not precisely reflect your views.

What You Might Achieve

With the help of concerned citizens, all state, regional, and local government agencies and most corporations should at least be capable of moving toward the following minimum climate-safety goals and policies:
- Purchasing all their power from renewable energy providers.
- Utilizing solar energy features in new buildings and retrofits.
- Upgrading lighting and appliances to more efficient types and models.
- Converting city and county motor vehicle fleets from ordinary internal combustion engines to more energy-efficient electric, hybrid-electric, natural gas, or (eventually) fuel cell propulsion.
- Supporting the expansion and improvement of energy-efficient mass transit, as well as telecommuting.
- Directing city and regional planners to deter urban sprawl by setting urban growth boundaries, building structures near public transit, encouraging multistoried construction, and using clustered development to maximize open space and preserve natural areas.

In the quest for community support and cooperation, it may be useful to set up an education task force together with representatives of local civic, community, and environmental organizations to coach key public officials on climate and energy issues.

The task force could provide officials with expert briefings and fact sheets as well as articles and books that put local energy and climate issues in a broad context. This patient work could have rich payoffs. Once public officials have been effectively briefed on issues and are paying attention to them, they may be receptive to new policy proposals.

If they do not respond, it may be useful to bring them petitions for action signed by their constituents. When even this is to no avail, citizens can sometimes get results by publicizing an official's views or voting record, or by volunteering for the campaign of a more enlightened opposing candidate. Local races can be decided by relatively few votes, and enthusiastic volunteers can often provide the margin of victory.

Federal and State Governments

Before attempting to lobby a legislative body, get acquainted with existing and proposed legislation by contacting one of the organizations listed on pages 127-130. For information about pending legislation, you may want to visit the Sierra Club's "vote watch" destination on the world wide web (www.SierraClub.org/votewatch). The Sierra Club's web site (www.SierraClub.org) will also give you information and contacts for the Club's chapters throughout the nation.

Once you're familiar with relevant Federal legislation, you can "weigh in" by calling your representative through the U.S. Capitol Switchboard at (202) 224-3121. Ask for your representative by name. When you're connected to his or her office, don't expect to reach him or her in person. A receptionist will take your call. To avoid becoming a tic mark on the rosters they keep of constituents' views, ask to speak to the legislative aide who handles the specific legislation or other issue about which you're calling.

In your discussion with the aide, let the aide know that you're a constituent and explain why you care about the issue. It will help to limit your call to a single issue and to convey a clear, concise message about it. Offer a convincing fact or two in support of your position. Provide additional information if you have it. Answer any questions honestly without invention and offer to obtain any additional information requested that you don't know. After the official has voted, you may want to follow up your call with a letter to the editor of the local newspaper publicizing the action, for better or worse.

In addition to calling the Capitol Switchboard, you can get direct dialing telephone numbers, mailing addresses, FAX numbers, and email addresses from the U.S. House and Senate web pages:

To contact your senators - http://www.senate.gov
To contact your representative - http://www.house.gov

These web pages also have biographies of the office holders and information about their committee assignments. Committee web pages can also be accessed from the House and Senate home pages.

Letters or telegrams (better) to members of Congress can be sent to:

The Honorable [Your Representative]
U.S. House of Representatives
Washington, D.C. 20515

The Honorable [Your Senator]
U.S. Senate
Washington, D.C. 20510

When you write, make your letter brief and specific. Proceed as if the person you are writing to is reasonable, honest, and of good will—even if that's not the case. "Respectfully yours," or the equivalent, is an appropriate closing.

You can also offer comments on Administration policies and priorities by contacting the White House:

White House Comment Line - (202) 456-1111
White House Fax Line - (202) 456-2461
The President's email - president@whitehouse.gov
The Vice President email - vice-president@whitehouse.gov

The White House
1600 Pennsylvania Avenue
Washington, DC 20500

The key Congressional committees with jurisdiction over energy, climate, and natural resource issues in Congress are:

For the Senate—	*For the House—*
Commerce, Science and Transportation	Transportation and Infrastructure

Energy and Natural Resources	Commerce
Appropriations	Appropriations
Environment and Public Works	International Relations
Finance	Science
Foreign Relations	Ways and Means

These committees are intensively lobbied by businesses and organizations but are not responsive to lobbying by citizens, except when the citizen also happens to be a committee member's constituent.

Committees with energy and climate jurisdiction vary in name from state to state, but most legislatures do have committees devoted to energy, natural resources, public utilities, and transportation, all of which loosely parallel state administrative agencies devoted to these matters.

To find direct channels of communication to your state decision makers, use a state government directory on-line or in the library, or contact a local reference librarian. But for a knowledgeable interpretation of the political landscape and its pressure points, you will want to consult the environmental and advocacy organizations who have been in the trenches on these issues.

Prominent organizations in each state are listed at the end of this chapter. You can also refer to the National Wildlife Federation's invaluable annual *Conservation Directory*, which lists over 3,000 conservation-oriented citizen organizations, government agencies, and college and universities (see http://www.nwf.org/ nwf/pubs/consdir/ index.html). Not only can these organizations tell you which office holders in your state have the greatest influence on energy and climate policies, but they can also tell you what bills are due for consideration. The League of Conservation Voters can provide you with officials' voting records on climate and energy.

In lobbying the state or Federal government, it is often helpful to tie your request to a local issue, such as the need to promote local economic development, create jobs, save on fuel bills, keep energy spending within the local area or the domestic economy, and protect natural resources from pollution.

The states and Federal government have various, usually under-funded programs that offer token support to efficiency and renewables. For example, states that have "public benefits funding" to support efficiency, renewables, and low-income weatherization have often set the corresponding levy to raise those funds at ridiculously low levels, measured in fractions of a tenth of a cent per kilowatt hour. Once you're familiar with these programs, you can advocate their expansion and modification.

When lobbying on the state and national level, the list of proposed policies outlined in chapter 6 may be a useful resource. Talk with lobbyists and other staff members of organizations already engaged on this issue for additional help.

What To Propose

In states that do not have laws and regulations corresponding to the policies outlined in chapter 6, citizens might propose state versions of these climate-safe policies wherever feasible, consistent with Federal regulations, which are sometimes preeminent. In states with generous endowments of a renewable resource—such as biomass, geothermal, hydro, solar, and wind—citizens may want to lobby for policies that favor the development of that resource.

If you live in an area known for outstanding wind resources, you might urge your legislators to strengthen local incentives for the manufacture and use of wind turbines as well as for advantageous net metering, transmission pricing, and power dispatch rules. Incentives might include state sales and property tax forgiveness for renewable energy projects as well as supplemental state wind energy production and investment tax credits and depreciation allowances. The American Wind Energy Association in Washington, D.C. can provide you with valuable background information on the costs as well as the economic and environmental benefits of wind turbines.

Similarly, if you live in an area with good solar resources, you might lobby your representatives for expanded solar energy production and investment tax credits applicable to solar thermal and solar electric technologies, as well as for favorable net metering arrangements. The American Solar Energy Society and the Solar Energy Industries Association could provide expert information and educational materials on these issues.

In western states with high-quality geothermal energy resources, you could advocate greater Federal and state investment in deep drilling technology that could one day make deep geothermal drilling to hot rock deposits feasible. The Geothermal Energy Association and the Geothermal Resources Council can help you with information and contacts.

In the Southeast, Northeast, and Midwest, where vast biomass resources exist, you might advocate biomass production incentives. The Biomass Energy Alliance or the National BioEnergy Industries Association can be of assistance. For guidance on how to be effective in supporting more efficient use of existing hydro facilities, contact the National Hydropower Association.

Local Lobbying

Whether you lobby a corporation, city council, school board, school, or school district, state educational system, transit district, city, state, or the Federal government itself, one important goal is to get the institution to adopt a comprehensive renewable energy and efficiency plan.

It is generally best to launch such campaigns by working with local chapters of environmental and community organizations or with qualified volunteers from the engineering community. You can try to forge alliances with community service organizations, religious groups, and community leaders. The efforts of broad-based community coalitions are difficult to ignore.

Making Contact in Your State

The list below identifies one or two organizations in each state that have been particularly knowledgeable and active on energy and climate issues. If you're interested in state-level action, all you need to do is contact one of these groups.

State	Organization • URL/Email Address	Telephone
Alabama	Alabama Environmental Council www.alenvironmentalcouncil.org	(202) 322-3126
Alaska	Alaska Conservation Alliance www.akvoice.org	(907) 258-6171
Arizona	Sierra Club, Phoenix Office www.sierraclub.org/chapters/az	(602) 253-8633
Arkansas	Arkansas Public Policy Panel appp@igc.org	(501) 376-7913 x12
California	Sierra Club, Sacramento Office www.motherlode.sierraclub.org	(916) 557-1100
Colorado	CO Public Interest Research Group www.pirg.org/copirg	(303) 573-7474 x313
	Sierra Club, Denver Office www.rmc.sierraclub.org	(303) 861-8819
Connecticut	CT Fund for the Environment dstrait@cfenv.org	(203) 787-0646
	CT Public Interest Research Group connpirg@pirg.org	(860) 233-7554
Delaware	Chesapeake Bay Foundation www.cbf.org	(301) 261-2350
Florida	Legal Envir. Assistance Foundation www.freenet.tlh.fl.us/LEAF	(941) 682-4991
	Sierra Club, St. Petersburg Office www.sierraclub.org/chapters/fl/suncoast/Suncoast.html	(727) 824-8813
Georgia	Sierra Club, Atlanta Office www.sierraclub.org/chapters/ga	(404) 888-9778
Hawaii	Sierra Club, Honolulu Office www.hi.sierraclub.org/	(808) 538-6616
Idaho	Sierra Club, Boise Office www.sierraclub.org/chapters/id/midsnake	(208) 384-1023
Illinois	Sierra Club, Chicago Office www.sierraclub.org/chapters/il	(312) 251-1680

Indiana	Hoosier Environmental Council	(317) 685-8800
	www.enviroweb.org/hecweb	
Iowa	Iowa Environmental Council	(515) 244-1194 x11
	www.earthweshare.org	
Kansas	Kansas Natural Resource Council	(785) 841-5902
	knrcsierra@cjnetworks.com	
Kentucky	No organization with a staffed office known to be active on climate and energy issues in the state.	
Louisiana	LA Environmental Action Network	(504) 928-1315
	www.leanweb.org	
Maine	Natural Resources Council of Maine	(207) 622-3101 x207
	www.nrcm.org	
Maryland	Chesapeake Bay Foundation	(301) 261-2350
	www.cbf.org	
Massachusetts	Sierra Club, Boston Office	(617) 742-2553
	www.members.tripod.com/masssierra	
Michigan	Michigan Environmental Council	(517) 487-9539
	www.mienv.org	
	Sierra Club, Lansing Office	(517) 484-2372
	www.sierraclub.org/chapters/mi	
Minnesota	MN Ctr. for Environmental Advocacy	(651) 223-5969
	mcea@mtn.org	
	Sierra Club, Minneapolis Office	(612) 379-3853
	www.northstar.sierraclub.org	
Mississippi	Sierra Club, Canton Office	(601) 352-1026
	www.sierraclub.org/chapters/ms	
Missouri	Sierra Club - Columbia Office	(573) 815-9250
	www.sierraclub.org/chapters/mo	
Montana	MT Environmental Information Ctr.	(406) 443-2520
	jjensen@meic.org	
Nebraska	Nebraska Wildlife Federation	(402) 994-2001
	dh43048@navix.net	
Nevada	No organization with a staffed office known to be active on climate and energy issues in the state.	
New Hampshire	Sierra Club, Concord Office	(603) 224-8222
	www.sierraclub.org/chapters/nh	
New Jersey	Sierra Club, Princeton Office	(609) 924-3141
	www.enviroweb.org/njsierra	
New Mexico	1000 Friends of New Mexico	(505) 848-8232
	nm1000@roadrunner.com	
New York	N.Y. Environmental Advocates	(518) 462-5526
	www.envadvocates.org	
	Sierra Club, Albany Office	(518) 426-9144
	www.sierraclub.org/chapters/ny	
North Carolina	Sierra Club, Raleigh Office	(919) 833-8467
	www.sierraclub-nc.org/capital	

North Dakota	Dakota Resource Council mtrechock@pop.ctctel.com	(701) 483-2851
Ohio	Ohio Environmental Council www.theoec.org	(614) 487-7506 x17
Oklahoma	Sierra Club, Oklahoma City Office www.sierraclub.org/chapters/ok/groups/okc	(405) 329-0412
Oregon	Oregon Environmental Council www.orcouncil.org	(503) 222-1963 x104
Pennsylvania	Sierra Club, Harrisburg Office www.sierraclub.org/chapters/pa/pinchot	(717) 232-1010
Rhode Island	Sierra Club, Providence Office www.ultranet.com/~clear/schome.html	(401) 521-4734
South Carolina	SC Coastal Conservation League NancyV@scccl.org	(843) 723-8035 x14
	Sierra Club, Columbia Office www.microbyte.net/sierra	(803) 256-8487
South Dakota	Sierra Club, Rapid City Office www.sierraclub.org/chapters/sd	(605) 348-1345
Tennessee	TN League of Conservation Voters www.lcvedfund.org	(615) 251-0309
Texas	Sierra Club, Austin Office www.sierraclub.org/chapters/tx/austin/index.html	(512) 476-6962
Utah	Sierra Club, Salt Lake City Office www.sierraclub.org/chapters/ut	(801) 467-9294
Vermont	Vermont Natural Resources Council www.vnrc.qpg.com	(802) 223-2328
Virginia	Sierra Club, Richmond Office www.sierraclubva.org	(804) 225-9113
Washington	Washington Environmental Council JoanCrooks@aol.com	(206) 622-8103
	Sierra Club, Seattle Office www.cascadechapter.org	(206) 523-7188 x2
West Virginia	WV Environmental Council www.wvecouncil.org/index.html	(304) 346-5891
Wisconsin	WI Environmental Decade Institute www.wsn.org	(608) 251-7020
	Sierra Club - Madison Office www.4lakes.org	(608) 256-0565
Wyoming	Wyoming Outdoor Council www.wocnet.org	(307) 332-7031

Appendix B: Frequently Asked Questions About Our Climate

How do we know what climate was like in the past?

Since thermometers didn't exist thousands of years ago, and no one kept temperature records, scientists studying past climates for clues to the future have relied on natural data instead. These climate-sensitive data are found in ice and coral cores, tree rings, bore holes in soil, sediments, ancient deposits of pollen in lake beds, evidence of glacier advance and recession, and the fossilized shells of tiny ancient marine life.

For example, scientists can now observe the effect carbon dioxide has had on the Earth's climate by examining ice cores taken from the polar regions. These cores contain trapped bubbles of ancient air that are analyzed for their carbon dioxide and oxygen levels, and then correlated with temperature data from other sources. These cores reveal a close connection between carbon dioxide and temperature for the past 420,000 years.

The shells of tiny sea creatures called foraminifera, recovered from seabed cores, contain two kinds of oxygen—oxygen-18 and lighter oxygen-16. When water evaporates from the oceans, the oxygen-16 water molecules evaporate at a greater rate. Thus, when foraminifera are found with relatively high oxygen-18 concentrations in their shells, we can infer they lived in a period when large amounts of water evaporated and were locked up in snow and ice, instead of returning as runoff to the ocean. That suggests these were periods of much glaciation.

Ancient fossilized pollen is also analyzed. From the abundance and distribution of plant species thus identified, we can infer what climate was like long ago. For the more recent record, the width of tree rings reveals growth rates, telling us which years were marked by high precipitation or drought. By correlating analyses of tree rings over large regions and eras, scientists can produce detailed information on historic precipitation and drought patterns.

Even very old and dead trees can be dated using radioactive carbon-14 as a clock. Carbon-14 decays at a known rate. So, by measuring the carbon-14 concentration left in a wood sample from a dead tree, scientists can determine when the tree died. By "working backward" from that date and counting annual tree rings, scientists can determine when droughts and precipitation occurred during the tree's lifetime.

Can We Prevent Climate Change By Planting Forests?

Until very recently, even many experts did not fully grasp the complex responses of forests to atmospheric changes and global temperature.

Before the Industrial Revolution, forests released about as much carbon into the air through respiration and decomposition as they withdrew through photosynthesis. Then, as the concentration of carbon dioxide in the air rose with industrialization, it helped stimulate the growth of trees and other plants because carbon dioxide acts as a fertilizer.

But a tree's response to progressively greater concentrations of carbon dioxide diminishes over time. Eventually, the addition of more carbon to our air will cease to boost the rate of forest growth. Meanwhile, global temperatures will continue to rise as atmospheric carbon increases.

Rising temperatures, in turn, will cause forest and soil respiration to increase very steeply. Carbon that lay stored in the soil over long periods will begin returning more rapidly to the atmosphere. In just a few decades, any benefits of a fertilizer effect from increased carbon dioxide will be stalled and overwhelmed by a dramatic rise in heat-trapping gas releases from the forest.

In addition, although the early stages of forest growth do remove large amounts of carbon from the air, as trees reach maturity, their growth naturally slows, and their rate of carbon absorption declines sharply. To keep pace with steadily rising industrial carbon emissions, vast new tracts of young forest would continually have to be created.

Moreover, forests are rarely secure from future development and other disturbance. They would have to be perpetually safeguarded from fire and other destruction, for when a forest burns or is devastated by insect infestation, the forest returns large amounts of stored carbon back to the atmosphere.

Therefore, although maintaining healthy forests does prevent a massive and premature release of carbon to the atmosphere, planting forests is still not a long-term solution to global warming. The only solution is to reduce carbon emissions.

How will global warming affect ocean currents?

The disruption of major ocean currents is one of the most disturbing potential consequences of rapid global warming. In a few areas of the North Atlantic, for example, the chilling of surface water causes a pronounced sinking of dense salty water toward the ocean bottom. (Cold water is denser than warm water, and saltwater is denser than freshwater.) Being lighter, freshwater from surface runoff and precipitation tends to float atop the salt water.

Far below the surface, the cold, dense salty current then flows south. This displacement of water produces a return current flowing north— the Gulf Stream— that brings western Europe its temperate weather. The entire system is known as the "conveyor belt circulation."

A critically important effect of global warming predicted by many scientific studies is a reduction in the strength of this circulation. That's because most climate models today indicate that as the Earth warms, precipitation will increase in high northern and high southern latitudes in winter. This would lead to an increase in the flow of fresh water into the North Atlantic, where the "downwelling" of salty water normally occurs. And when too much fresh water replaces the salty surface water layer, the conveyor belt circulation will weaken and may ultimately halt altogether.

Stoppages of the conveyor belt circulation have occurred in the past 100,000 years, sometimes with frightening speed in periods as short as several years. If a collapse occurs again, the climate of Europe could be altered dramatically. One climate model simulation shows that the northern Atlantic would then be ice-covered to south of Iceland. That would mean enormous environmental, economic, and social changes for Europe, and even for the U.S., as Europe's trading partner.

Several scientific research teams have recently found evidence that part of the oceanic conveyor belt—the North Atlantic Drift current—already is being disrupted by an increase of freshwater to the Arctic Ocean.

What is "climate change feedback"?

A feedback loop occurs when a process initiates a secondary process that either amplifies it (positive feedback) or diminishes it (negative feedback). Thus, a positive climate feedback occurs when the release of heat-trapping gases sets in motion processes that result in a still greater release of heat-trapping gases. In this way, a relatively small initial increase in heat-trapping gas can be magnified and may produce a large impact.

A common example of a positive climate feedback involves water vapor. The higher the Earth's temperature gets, the more water will evaporate. More water in the atmosphere will, in turn, tend to trap more outward-bound heat and warm the Earth even further.

By contrast, if something were to cause enough global cooling so that more snow and ice formed over less reflective surfaces (such as a vegetated area), this would increase the reflectance of incoming radiation back into space and would cool the Earth still further, amplifying the original cooling—another form of positive feedback.

A negative feedback would counter warming with cooling, or vice versa. Thus positive feedbacks can be highly destabilizing to the climate, while negative ones are generally stabilizing.

Appendix C: Selected Bibliography

Berger, John J. *Charging Ahead: The Business of Renewable Energy and What it Means to America.* Berkeley, CA: University of California Press, 1997.

Gelbspan, Ross. *The Heat Is On: The High Stakes Battle Over Earth's Threatened Climate.* Reading, MA: Perseus, 1998.

Houghton, John T. *Global Warming: The Complete Briefing.* Cambridge, England: Cambridge University Press, 1997.

Intergovernmental Panel on Climate Change, Contribution of Working Group III. *Climate Change 1995: Economic and Social Dimensions of Climate Change.* J.P. Bruce, H. Lee, and E.F.Haites (eds.). Cambridge, England: Cambridge University Press, 1996.

Intergovernmental Panel on Climate Change, Contribution of Working Group II. *Climate Change 1995—Impacts, Adaptations and Mitigation of Climate Change: Scientific-Technical Analyses.* Cambridge, England: Cambridge University Press, 1996.

Intergovernmental Panel on Climate Change. *Climate Change 1995: The Science of Climate Change.* Cambridge, England: Cambridge University Press, 1996.

Office of Utility Technologies, Energy Efficiency and Renewable Energy and Electric Power Research Institute. *Renewable Energy Technology Characterizations.*TR-109496. Washington D.C: U.S Department of Energy, and Palo Alto, CA: EPRI, December 1997.

Schneider, Stephen H. *Laboratory Earth: The Planetary Gamble We Can't Afford to Lose.* New York: Basic Books/HarperCollins, 1997.

A comprehensive list of books, websites, organizations, and other valuable resources about global climate change and clean energy may be found at the *Beating the Heat* web site: www.berkeleyhills.com/beatingtheheat.

Index

About the Author

John J. Berger is an independent energy and environmental consultant. He has worked for the National Research Council of the National Academy of Sciences, corporations such as Lockheed and Chevron, nonprofit groups, and governmental organizations, including the U. S. Congress.

Dr. Berger's popular writing on energy and natural resource issues has appeared in the *Los Angeles Times,* the *Boston Globe,* and many other publications. He is the author or editor of seven books on climate, nuclear and renewable energy, environmental restoration, and forestry. They include: *Understanding Forests* (Sierra Club Books, 1998), *Charging Ahead. The Business of Renewable Energy and What It Means for America* (Henry Holt and Co., 1997/University of California Press, 1998), and *Restoring the Earth: How Americans Are Working to Restore Our Damaged Environment* (Alfred A. Knopf, 1985/Doubleday, 1987).

Dr. Berger holds a bachelor's degree in political science from Stanford University, a master's degree in energy and natural resources from the University of California, Berkeley, and a Ph.D. in ecology from the University of California, Davis. He has taught at the Graduate School of Public Affairs of the University of Maryland and now lives with his family in El Cerrito, California. He can be reached at LSA Associates, 157 Park Place, Point Richmond, CA 94801. Phone: (510) 231-7714.